YOUR FIRST SIX FIGURES:

Eight Keys to Unlock Freedom, Flow and Financial Success with Your Online Business

JENN SCALIA

Your First Six Figures: Eight Keys to Unlock Freedom, Flow
and Financial Success with Your Online Business

©2018 Jenn Scalia.

ISBN-13: 978-1985607651

ISBN-10: 1985607654

Contents

Foreward

If you've picked up this book, there's a very good chance you are what I would call "one of us".

One of the ones who, since the earliest of early ages, and perhaps before you can even really remember, felt the call.

The call of more...

The call of purpose...

The call of destiny...

The call of LIFE, whispering, coaxing, guiding, even COMMANDING, and telling you, "Hey, you! Yes, you! There's more...you were born for more...more is AVAILABLE...won't you come and get it?"

For those who grew up with this call, the voice was barely more than a niggle, a little something we felt amongst all of the usual pressures of growing up, pursuing good things as an adult, doing what we were meant to do, and creating a life.

At some point though, something happened. Perhaps you just woke up differently. All of a sudden, you realised:

"I'm not going to live the normal life.

I'm going to do something different.

I'm going to do something *extraordinary*."

And maybe even this, as audacious and daring and unrealistic as it seemed to be—

"I'm going to have it ALL!"

Of course you had no idea HOW on earth you were indeed going to do all of that, or even where to begin, but something within you just knew—

"Yes. Success is my freakin' BIRTHRIGHT."

If this is you, if you're nodding your head and resonating with even part of what I'm saying, then here's what I want you to know:

Jenn Scalia?

This woman is the woman who is going to show you not only just how available your dreams are (very available!), but also exactly how you can bring them to life.

Even if you are just getting started...not even started...or have no clue where to start!

How can I be so sure, about Jenn?

I was fortunate enough to meet Jenn when she was still in the earlier phases of her online business, building what is now unarguably one of THE most powerful female entrepreneur brands online.

It's funny because, at the time, energetically I really didn't realise just how early on Jenn was in paving her way and leaving behind a life that had NOT given her what she desired and knew she could have.

All I saw was this powerhouse of a woman who knew what she wanted, was determined to get it, and was filled with deep compassion and a desire to help others also break free of the norm.

I saw in her a lot of what I know people see in ME, and no doubt in YOU, also:

This is somebody who will do what it takes.

This is somebody who was born for more.

This is somebody who is a natural LEADER.

And hot damn—this is somebody with drive, determination, and focus which is almost scary.

In other words—ONE OF US.

Over the next few years, I was fortunate to get to know Jenn very well. She became a private client, we eventually met in person, and of course a friendship developed as well.

It wasn't until even recently that it really clicked for me just how fast Jenn built her business and brand to epic leader status, and how the reason that came about was because she simply didn't allow for anything less. This, plus the heart and soul and PURPOSE she bring to her work and her message, makes for a very rare mix and one which, quite simply, stands out and is an honour to even be around.

I had the biggest smile ever on my face as I dived in to read this book, and there were many moments where I had to shake my head in wonder at how Jenn has taken what is a pretty huge topic (and also a somewhat "mystical" one for a lot of people) and broken it down into something that is not only ACTIONABLE for you, but also hugely inspiring and entertaining to read.

I know you're going to love this book and feel your mind expanded over and over again with what's possible for you.

But if you apply even a percentage of it?

I know it's going to change your life.

Happy reading!

And remember—

Life is Now. Press Play.

Kat x

Katrina Ruth (Kat Loterzo)

www.thekatrinaruthshow.com

INTRODUCTION

The Only Way Out

The door behind her slammed so loud that the echo drummed in her ears for a whole minute afterwards.

Alarmed by the abrupt shove she had just received, it took her body a while to adjust its balance to this new rigid position.

To move her arms and legs—nothing but pain, thanks to the numerous bruises that so cruelly decorated her skin. Some were fresh, others ancient.

Tears drenched her face. Her heart rate soared. Clenched fists turned her knuckles white.

"Where am—"

She caught herself.

She knew. Many times before, she'd been here in this room.

Each time she returned, her promise to herself was the same: "Never again!"

Yet here she was.

The room was so dark that she kept her hands pressed to the wall, her fingertips brushing slowly along to guide her slowed stride.

She remained hunched over, her ability to stand erect seized from her.

Slowly, she managed to move through the darkness. She felt cold metal.

"A doorknob?" *She latched on with both hands.* "A doorknob!"

Relief radiated through her body, numbing the worst of her pain.

Hoping and praying that escape was imminent, she opened the door...slowly.

A crack of light struck her face. As her eyes adjusted, she saw a sign above the door.

"Relationship."

Her heart sank. Now, light illuminated her black and blue skin—the road map of her story into this oppressive room.

What she thought was a new way out was, in fact, an all-too-familiar door. She had walked through it before many times, experiencing everything that lie beyond— both the joys and pains of the "R" word.

Love brought overwhelming happiness and inconsolable sorrow—but every relationship was biased towards the latter of the two. At the end of each "us" this woman had known, escape from dysfunction had somehow ushered her back to this same dark place.

Shaking away the memories, she pushed the door shut and boldly faced the darkness.

THE ONLY WAY OUT

"Not this time."

She wasn't going to be tricked again. Darkness was more welcoming than the light of hopelessness.

Determined to continue down her chosen path, her right hand became her trusted guide—the wall, her necessary support.

Abruptly, she halted at the next door. Much like the last one, she opened it slowly. Gone were the days of embracing modes of escape without caution.

A reflection of light revealed the sign.

"Job."

She couldn't help but chuckle.

Then came a slow shake of the head. She barely took a pause before slamming that door shut.

Years of labor without fulfillment, and long hours without fair compensation devastated her mind and body.

"Never again. Never, EVER again."

Before moving on to what came next—whatever that would be—she paused.

She felt something happening inside her. Rather, she noticed what wasn't *happening.*

Refusing the escapes offered by the last two doors brought no fear, no regret. Instead she felt the embrace of an old and dear friend.

Confidence.

Her arm that once limply guided her now extended with power. Her speed quickened. Opening and closing the next three doors felt almost passive.

"School."

Slam.

"Affirmation."

Slam.

"Middle Class."

Slam.

After swinging that fifth door closed as fast as she'd opened it, a light unseen revealed a truth so simple it made her smile.

Never before had she spent so much time in this darkness. And the longer she persisted in this journey of courage, the less it felt like one.

Without needing the wall to guide her, she charged ahead, arms by her side.

"Done..." *The only word that could describe her feeling.* "Done!"

Done going through doors that lead to disappointment.

Done going through doors that lead to rejection.

Done going through doors...period.

Yes, the doors of escape—and their promises of quick and easy freedom—were attractive at first. They always are.

THE ONLY WAY OUT

Marriage...

A middle class income...

A college degree...

Applause from others...

A stable 9-to-5 job...

These all once seemed like simple solutions, easy escapes from darkness and doubt.

But the slow pulses of each ache and bruise reminded her—"Don't go back. NEVER go back."

There in the darkness, alone with her thoughts, she filtered out no idea that revealed itself.

From here, she could return to one of the five doors and suffer a slow and silent death of the person she would have otherwise become. Potential unmet, purpose forfeited.

She could take a seat in the darkness until it felt comfortable enough to call home. Although her fate would be the same, at least the withdrawal from reality would keep her mind, body and spirit from receiving another round of battering.

Or...she could say, "Fuck it."

Instead of waiting for the right door to appear, she could create her own—no, she would *create her own!*

She would make her own door of escape—and not one of escape from, *but escape* to.

No more than a second passed before she made up her mind.

This final decision brought a surge of energy, forcing her spine upwards. She stood erect for the first time in years, with no thought to the faint pain of bruises.

With the strength of an Amazon, she thrust a fist into the wall. It gave way, brittle as thin ice at winter's last thaw.

Her life's purpose motivating her, she worked and scraped and pulled and tugged until a peep of light grew into the rays of a sunrise.

A burst of fresh air filled her lungs with the hope of a new way of life.

"Freedom." *She breathed it in deep.*

Then the moment of truth came—she realized that the door she had fashioned with her own two hands was more than a hole in the wall, it was a passageway.

A passageway for others to follow, and they—like her—would never be the same again after tasting this sweet air upon their tongues.

"Freedom."

This story may seem like a fictional account of an unnamed girl. In fact, what you just read is my story.

For too many years, I wasted away in the darkness. But it was at one of the lowest points of my life that I finally chose to reject the five doors life presented to me once and for all.

THE ONLY WAY OUT

I had endured exactly seven months without steady paychecks. My killer marketing job at one of the largest casino resorts in Atlantic City, gone without warning.

"Laid off."

The bills piled up. Creditors came calling. Rarely did my bank account rise above the negative. Free-lancing gigs and a desperate attempt at real estate barely made ends meet for my family.

Money wasn't the only problem. Every other part of my life lay in pieces, with no hope of re-creating a puzzle even remotely resembling my hopes and dreams.

My marriage, my relationships, my sanity—gone.

Every waking hour, which included most of them past midnight, I spent trying to figure out my purpose. That adventure took the form of a single question I had no answer to.

"Who the hell am I?"

Every "supposed to" I knew of, I was doing. But I still saw nothing—nothing but darkness.

For so long, I was surrounded by people who were content with mediocrity, satisfied with an average life or below. And that's what I learned to aspire for—comfort, simplicity, normal.

But the more I explored, the fewer answers I had—and I had started this with none! Nowhere I looked did I see happiness. Not in my friends' lives. Not in my relatives', husband's or in-laws'.

Everyone did what they *had* to do just to scrape by, calling it a day when "just good enough" was...just good enough.

Long hours at thankless jobs brought them more stress than joy. Nevertheless, they stayed employed, celebrating each work anniversary by getting punch-drunk.

This never made sense to me. Even though I found myself growing up in an upper middle class two-parent home, something about me was different.

"The black sheep." An outcast. That girl who always saw things differently. I bet you can imagine the issues this caused during my late teens and early twenties!

For all the years before and for many years after, I continued to check off the box next to every "should" in my life.

Go to school...get a job...get married...have a baby...live happily ever after...

I tried them all and succeeded before age 30.

Except for the most important one—*happily ever after*.

My college days were short lived, sacrificed in favor of young love. Several (unsatisfying) jobs followed, along with two marriages and a baby.

Something was missing, but it might as well have been everything. I had no idea where to start or how to find "me."

THE ONLY WAY OUT

With each passing year, the grim reality of my choices revealed itself more and more.

"None of this is ever going to make you happy."

My true purpose lay undiscovered, though I knew by then what it *wasn't*.

The easier choice would have been to accept my lot in life as just an average girl from a small town. I was lucky, right? Most women my age would kill to have what I took for granted.

In those days of indecision, my confidence was undoubtedly bipolar. Some days, I thought I was amazing, the next day—not so much. One thing I did know—I was now an expert at letting outside influences change my view of myself, my purpose and where I was headed in life.

I was constantly reaching. Reaching for something I had no clue about. Whatever it was, it certainly couldn't be found in my current situation. I knew I had to change that. I had to pull the trigger. I had to take the leap if I ever wanted more out of life.

Time and time again, fear of the unknown held me back. Yet deep down, I knew I was above average. I think we all are, actually. The fact is, we are all pushed down to a lower level day after day by the people who raise us, and then by the people we surround ourselves with as we age.

Most people accept what I just described as "life." They live it. Then they die—little by little with each passing day until they accept the mediocrity as a so-called "blessing in disguise."

Not me.

In my heart, I nurtured a belief that came to defeat all others, that I would not live—or die—average. Somehow, some way, I would break the barriers of the mundane and live an amazing life. No one could stop me from that destiny!

Except...myself.

So there I was—broke, hopeless and alone at a point in my life where I "should" have had it all together. Truth be told, at some point I did have it all together—until I decided to fuck shit up and not be normal.

But when you imagine living the same monotonous life decade after decade until 40, 50, 60 years have passed—you cannot help but refuse to stomach that future as inevitable. At that point, there is no reason to *not* fuck shit up!

In my routine, I did whatever it took to please others, to make people like me, to find acceptance—however shallow it was. Then I got tired. Tired of playing an assiduous game that didn't serve me—AT ALL. It didn't make me any happier, make anyone like me or want me more, and it didn't propel me into my purpose.

So why was I doing it? The same reason most people continue to do things that are ingrained in their psyche. Limiting beliefs—a lot of them.

Limited beliefs in every single area of my life—from relationships to money, from parenting to my career, from religion to my entire view of who I was as a human being.

For a while I struggled in limbo between what I *wanted* to do, and what I was *supposed* to do.

THE ONLY WAY OUT

The day I decided that door number six would be one I created myself was the day I literally woke up and said, *"FUCK IT!"*

"I'm DONE! I'm done living my life for everyone else."

The fear inside me met its match. I was ready to slap on the boxing gloves and go toe to toe with the only enemy that could stop me—me.

"Now or never."

The more I kept putting it off, the easier it would be to convince myself that normal was acceptable.

But it isn't. And it wasn't.

I went out on a limb and made that limb my headquarters. I diverted all the energy being wasted on wallowing in negative emotions and trying to control uncontrollable situations into my drive to find greatness—wherever it was, whatever the cost.

When I stand before crowds of thousands today, I tell them the truth—my life today isn't an accident. My purpose isn't an accident. And you reading my story at this very moment—this is certainly no accident.

Was it easy? Hell no!

But once I made the decision to find my own way out of the darkness, it wasn't exactly hard either. A word to the wise though—the toughest part is going against the grain, going against everything you've ever been taught, against the wishes of parents, family and friends, against what feels like a quick escape.

Once I conquered this resistance, I was able to overcome anything life threw at me. No longer was I a slave to everyone else's ideals and insecurities. My message became so clear, and my passion so unbridled. No one could stop me anymore—not even myself.

And the naysayers? They found themselves so enthralled by what I had done that they wanted a piece of the action, too.

So what about you? What is your story?

Are you in the dark room like I was, looking for a way of escape?

If you can relate to any aspect of my story, then I have good news for you—I have 8 doors ready for, with 8 corresponding keys.

Not only will these doors release you from the prison of darkness, they will open a way to ultimate success—so you can finally live the life of your dreams.

If you follow my practical steps and apply my time-tested tools, you will experience a life filled with purpose and contentment that are completely yours—and no one else's.

I don't just share my story for me; I want you to believe that more is possible for anyone, no matter how dire and hopeless the situation. Average is not what you have to call home if you don't want to. It doesn't matter what phase of life you are in—married, single, divorced, a mom, childless, unemployed, middle class job.

THE ONLY WAY OUT

Wherever your next step needs to lead you, the information among these pages will help you get there.

So keep reading, grab each key I give you and stick with me as we journey out of the darkness and into the only way out.

CHAPTER 1

Your New Operating System

Mindset over mechanics is what leads to real, true and lasting success.

At this point in a business book, you expect the author go on some long, drawn-out story about how they built a successful business, made millions working a handful of hours a week and retired to a beach with endless margaritas.

But I'm not that type of author.

Thousands of entrepreneurs all over the world know me for my tough love, no-bullshit style. That means this book is not about me, it's about YOU.

In the pages that follow, we are going to uncover your biggest fears and empower you to share your message with the world—even if you feel trapped right now in a darkness like the one I spent so many years trying to escape from.

What you'll get from my book is a fluff-free path through 8 doors. I will give you every secret and every key that took me from being a broke single mom to where I am today—a 7-figure business owner, bestselling author of *Against the Grain* (co-authored with speaker Brian Tracy) and a household name in the online business community.

One of the most important things I stress in my brand is building (and maintaining) trust. The truth is, a lot of get rich quick types only care about the first part—building trust, but only until the sale is made and they've got your money. Their rags-to-riches success stories are totally self-serving and are meant to stir up jealousy. Not cool.

We're different. You and I are on a journey together, first through the door with the sign "Your New Operating System" - a concept brought to light by one of my most influential mentors, Jesse Elder, and then through the remaining seven.

In the Introduction, I shared my story with you because you need to know something:

I've been right where you are.

Even after I created my way of escape from the darkness, things weren't easy—not at first. For the first 18 months of "Jenn Scalia Inc." that woman was broke! I had no clients and no money.

I did have memberships in all the popular online business programs, so I thought I was doing all the right things. But no one knew who I was. Back then, my current tagline "It's time the world knows your name!" was my own personal fantasy.

When I took a magnifying glass to my business to figure out where my success blocks were, I realized that my magnifying glass was a mirror.

It was me. *I* was the problem. It wasn't my lack of business savvy or know-how keeping me stuck, small and seriously underpaid.

It was my mindset—how I thought about who I was supposed to be and what I was supposed to do as an online entrepreneur.

None of the experts I followed warned me about a faulty mindset. It was the missing piece of my success formula. Maybe it is for you, too—that's why we are covering mindset here in Chapter 1.

For example, if you subconsciously doubt that you can ever have a sustainable business, you will manifest feast-or-famine income cycles. I PROMISE you I will not stand by and let that happen.

Because I've been there. *Never again.*

You don't have to be either.

Ready to start a revolution?

We're going to start with un-fucking your mindset. Let's face it, if you're constantly sizing yourself up against others and feeling like you're never good enough, your business has no chance.

What happens between our ears makes all the difference. It certainly did for me, and I know it can for you, too.

It's NOT going to happen overnight, and we'll be putting in some SERIOUS work together. But it will happen. Your new mindset will keep you on track so that you apply everything you learn in this book.

The results will be amazing.

YOUR NEW OPERATING SYSTEM

Like I said, it all starts with mindset. If you aren't where you want to be or struggle with inconsistent income, the likelihood is that 99% of the blame falls on you and what you believe about yourself and what you can achieve.

Every mindset is an Operating System (OS). Like an actual Operating System for your smartphone or tablet, your mindset determines what you are allowed to do, what capabilities you have.

By the end of this chapter, you'll have an entirely new Operating System for your life and business that makes success inevitable. This will change the entire framework of how you operate and will leave you with a new foundation to build your business upon that isn't made out of a scarcity, "chase them clients down" mentality. Instead, you'll be living and working from a place of strength.

First off, to make a big income and create a big impact, some internal work is required. Every mindset has two aspects: there is what mindset causes you to *be*, and there is what mindset causes you to *do*.

Let's start with being.

Like iOS or Android or Windows 7, you can't install the newest version, try it out for a few days, uninstall it, then freak out because all the new features are gone.

That's YOUR own damn fault!

In the same way, a new mindset isn't something you start to create when you're reading a book (like this one), forget about it when you're done and then wonder why you're not seeing the results you hoped for.

YOUR FIRST SIX FIGURES

That would be like walking through the first door to freedom, then going right back into the darkness.

For your new mindset to take effect, you need to commit to using your new Operating System every day. Yes there IS a learning curve—just like when you upgrade to iOS 8 after you've used iOS 7 for a while.

Once you develop a practice to help maintain your new mindset, things will change rapidly. I'm talking about committing to a DAILY practice. Over time, you'll raise your vibration and put yourself in the state of receiving all that you want—the connections, the opportunities, the clients, the raving fans.

But remember, this has to be done daily to re-program your old beliefs. Don't let that old Operating System reinstall itself!

Your daily practice can include activities like gratitude journaling (more on this later) or meditation or prayer or yoga. As long as what you're doing shifts your feelings about yourself and your business, stay with it. Be consistent. You can't just do it once or a few times a week and expect it to have amazing results.

I don't want you sitting around for one or two hours every day just thinking happy thoughts either. There has to be a purpose to your consistent practice. When I said that your new OS is a way of thinking, it's not just HOW you think, it's also WHAT you think.

Your OS is going to be based in large part on answers to the most important questions a business owner can ask. These are questions you need to answer for yourself because your OS is YOURS, not mine. I'm going to show you how to create an OS that works for you, just as I created one that works for me and got me to where I am now.

The questions to answer are short, but your answers can be as long, detailed and thorough as you want.

What are you here for?

Yes, a simple question. Obvious answers might immediately come to mind like "To help others and really make an impact," or "To be the best version of myself I can be."

Dig beneath the surface. Go deep into your essence. What is your fundamental desire? It's not just about making money in your business.

In other words, what is the REAL reason you do the work you do?

What opportunities do you see in the world that you—with your skills, abilities and knowledge—are perfectly suited for?

Get this answer right, and you'll have a powerful tool to add to your daily practice. You'll be constantly reminding yourself why you do what you do, and your approach to everything will change. You'll feel a new life come into even routine activities, like posting daily on your social media channels or creating new opt-in pages to A/B test.

As a result of knowing what you are here for, your outcomes in business will change for the better dramatically as well.

What do you stand for?

Your answers to this second question, combined with those for the first question, are like a one-two punch that forces fear, anxiety and doubt out of your business.

You've heard the cliché, "She who stands for nothing will fall for anything"? That was me for the first months of my business. Because I only knew that I was in business to make money, I looked at the experts of online business and tried to be like them.

Don't be a copycat—I realized that before it was too late. Now, I have a brand no one can duplicate.

All because I chose to stand for something. I stand for being authentic, for being REAL with my tribe, for challenging the status quo, for telling it like it is, for giving tough love and calling people on their shit.

Within weeks of making the choice to stand for what mattered to me, I found opportunities open up by the hundreds—new ways to share my message, to write for publications that influence the masses, to appear on podcasts and shows that put me in front of hundreds of thousands of potential customers.

Most importantly, I was creating conflict. I now knew what I stood for. That also meant I knew what I stood AGAINST—the get rich quick biz types, promises of overnight success without any effort and fluff-filled programs and courses that get people all hyped up but leave them directionless.

To say this ruffled some feathers is putting it lightly. But you stir up interest when you create conflict.

YOUR NEW OPERATING SYSTEM

In other words, you know you've got it right when some people don't like it.

Your opposition may be the haters who troll YouTube comments sections or they could be family members and friends. Regardless, when you announce that you're going to stand for career freedom, that you're not going to go the way of mediocrity, that you're going to do whatever it takes to grow a business...

You'll ruffle feathers. You'll turn up noses. And you'll upset the apple cart.

Do you know what I say to that?

FUCK the apple cart!

You are meant for MORE than being average, sister. So what do you stand for? What do you stand against? What controversy or conflict are you willing to stir up—because it's who you are, because it's the right thing to do?

Write your answers down and review them daily as part of your practice.

And don't forget—if you stand for nothing, no one will stand with you.

Speaking of standing with you, you must stand for yourself and hold firm to an unwavering belief in your gifts and talents FIRST. Whenever I begin work with a new student, one of the first things I direct them to do is write down ALL of the amazing things about them.

Seriously. All of it.

YOUR FIRST SIX FIGURES

All of the accomplishments, wins, amazing characteristics and traits, what they excel at, their strengths and more.

Once we realize just how amazing we are and start celebrating even the smallest of wins, it becomes much easy to sell ourselves to prospective clients.

So Instead of constantly comparing yourself to other entrepreneurs who "seem" smarter or richer or more successful, take a look inside, discover your strengths and use that to fuel your motivation and supercharge your success.

Ultimately, we have to sell ourselves on ourselves first. Before anyone else will believe it...YOU have to.

Comparing your brand to the most popular ones in the industry subconsciously forces you to be like them, look like them, sound like them. But more of them same is EXACTLY what repels potential clients from you!

By updating your Operating System, you will become irreplaceable. This is SO important that I teach every new student in my program *Captivate* to step out of the traditional box of "supposed to's" in their industry so they can shine as who they are. Not as clones of everyone else in their niche.

Toward the beginning of this chapter, I wrote that there are two aspects to your new mindset, your new OS—what mindset causes you to *be*, and what mindset causes you to *do*.

Now that you've begun to answer the questions that define who you will *be* in business and in life, let's dive deep into the second aspect.

YOUR NEW OPERATING SYSTEM

Remember the Operating System analogy—an OS on your computer allows you to do only that which it allows you to do. Your mindset is the same. It allows you to achieve whatever your mindset is compatible with.

If smashing your income ceiling is not part of your mindset, guess what? You'll never shatter your own personal income record. Your mindset just won't let it happen.

That's why whenever I discuss mindset on a podcast, a guest spotlight or in some other media appearance, you'll always hear me say, "Your mindset is your reality."

And when I say that your mindset defines what you *do*, I mean that as what you do for YOU—but also what you do for the WORLD.

It's "both/and" because your life isn't lived in a vacuum. Your business doesn't operate in one either.

What separates you from the get rich quick biz types is the big vision your mindset gives you. You're here to make an actual impact, not sell 100 licenses to a product a month for $1,000 a piece. There is MORE to your business than the end result of producing a profit.

That's why creating a mission statement to define your big vision is one of the most powerful things you can ever do to make your new mindset stick. The clarity we will create from this exercise will cement the foundation of your belief in yourself in a way that people cannot ignore.

Writing down answers to the questions below will turn ideas you have for your big vision into a habit—and that is how you make your business an unstoppable force in your industry.

You must have a clear vision of what you want to achieve. If you want to experience things differently than what you've been experiencing, you have to get clear on what you want and what you don't want.

I'll get you started. Grab a journal and find a quiet place where you can be undistracted for about 10 minutes. Answer these questions like the future of your business depends on it (because it does):

- What impact do you want to make?
- How do you want the world to change because of the work that you've done?
- What do you want most from your business? Why are you doing this?
- Do you desire freedom, a specific lifestyle, travel or a boatload of cash?
- Write out your current reality. Be honest with yourself. You can't change what you aren't willing to acknowledge.
- Now write out the reality you desire for your business. $10K months? $100,000 launches? Fully booked with perfect clients who pay premium prices and pay on time? Write it out in the present tense like your vision has already come to pass.
- Set the intention that you will make your "new reality" happen.
- Repeat this "new reality" to yourself daily as part of your practice, until you really believe that it will happen. Believing that we can actually achieve our vision is the next step towards success.

As you go through that exercise, your income will come up over and over.

YOUR NEW OPERATING SYSTEM

Let's face it—those of us don't want to follow the tired path of school-job-retirement aren't flocking to entrepreneurship because we want to make *less* money.

We're here for more—a LOT more. If I asked any of my co-workers at old jobs if they could ever imagine earning $10,000 a month, they'd laugh me out of their cubicle and wonder what illegal business transactions I had in mind.

If I asked the same question about $100,000 a month, I would get not much more than an eye roll and a "Keep on dreaming, Jenn," dismissal.

Because many of us come from the 9 to 5 world, we have to shake off that kind of limited thinking.

If you're going to smash your invisible income ceiling, you have to realize that you're operating with set limits on what you think you can earn. In my very first year in business, I hoped to earn near my typical salary of $40,000.

Guess what! In my first year in business, I earned $35,000—that was my cap! I hadn't yet cultivated a 6-figure or 7-figure mindset (or even figured out how to).

To choose a mindset that matches your income level is one of the hardest parts of the entrepreneurial journey because it requires letting go of what has been comfortable but not profitable. I know because that's what I had to do.

Like I say to every incoming student of *Captivate*, "If you want to generate 6-figures, you CANNOT and WILL NOT be able to do it with a 4-figure mindset." I know because I was living proof!

YOUR FIRST SIX FIGURES

One realization that kicked my income-earning ass into high gear was calculating the COST of not living up to who I wanted to be. For example, if your goal is to have a $10k month but you only make $5k, then 3 months later you've lost $15k. One of the best lessons I ever learned in business came from my trusted and loved mentor Jesse Elder, he told me that the most expensive thing in your business is the money you are NOT making.

The bottom line is that when you aren't hitting your exact income goals month after month, you are losing.

After I recognized the artificial income limit that my old salary was hanging over my head, I knew I had no choice but to do whatever it took to obliterate my limit.

The next year in business, I increased my revenue by 1400%! I went from making $35K to $500K in one year, then soaring well over 7-figures in revenue the very next year. We only get what we believe we deserve. We all have the potential to be where we want to be.

For some, it's hard to reach those monthly goals because you're not focused on doing the right things that will get you there. Maybe you're not working hard enough on the right things, or working too hard on the wrong things. If you're operating from a place of lack, thinking only about how much money you're *not* making, then you'll get more of what you focus on—nothing. That's why we worked through the process of creating your new Operating System in this chapter before I ever said a word about money.

As you set sight on goals higher than any you've ever set before, much less *met*, you'll find your mindset expanding. It WON'T feel stupid to say out loud, "I'm the type of person who consistently earns ten thousand dollars a month," or whatever your goal is.

Thinking bigger is all it takes.

I'm going to give you a number.

$60,000.

What is this number?

I'll tell you what it's *not*—how much money I made this month.

No, $60K is how much money I spend in 2 months to grow my 7-figure business.

I'm not even going to imagine what my old co-workers would think about that.

The truth is, your new Operating System should NOT be all about the hustle. I'm all for bootstrapping and DIY-ing as much as possible when you're starting out. But if you want a mental Operating System that results in multiple 6-figure launches or high 5-figure months, you've got to think bigger. Your first 6 figures is the hardest because you're stretching your beliefs about what is possible for you.

As you can see, entrepreneurship isn't all rainbows, butterflies, vacations and cash. It's about investing—spending money to make money.

If you who want to go BIG and have $25K, $50K or $100K months, you're going to have to invest like you mean it.

YOUR FIRST SIX FIGURES

It's imperative to start making decisions as the person you WANT to be, not the person you are today. If you keep making choices from where you are right now, you will continue to be that person.

Investing in yourself wisely is simultaneously one of the most overlooked AND misunderstood skills I believe every entrepreneur needs. Yes, I do mean SKILL. Because knowing what to invest when and how much is teachable, which is why I spend so much time covering it in *Captivate*.

Would you spend $1 to earn $100 more? I would. And I did.

For example, that $60K I mentioned earlier got put to use for:

- Running, building, maintaining and improving my website
- Hiring a team (Virtual Assistant, Online Business Manager, Copywriter, Web Designer)
- My own education, training and mentoring to improve the skills I already have
- Legal, accounting and bank fees
- Office supplies, client gifts and postage
- Monthly business subscriptions for storage, hosting, email marketing, contracts and scheduling
- Advertising expenses to reach a larger and wider audience

When you make outsourcing a necessity within your business model, there is no limit to what you can earn.

Many of my readers will get so inspired by this example that they feel like tossing my book aside right now to get back to work. Others will be more like my old co-worker and doubt themselves.

Maybe you really, REALLY want to smash your income ceiling and set a new upper limit on what is possible (and then smash that new limit). Maybe you plateaued around $2K, $3K or $5K per month.

I'm not going to scold you and claim that your goal needs to be higher, more like $20K or $30K a month.

I want to stretch you, not make you set a goal so unrealistically high that you don't have the joy of conquering other goals on the way, like $7.5K or $10K.

Maybe your goal is just to make $5,000 a month consistently and replace the current income you are making at a 9 to 5. That's perfectly okay.

Whatever blocks you DO have, I want you to be aware of them—and CRUSH them.

A couple of years ago, I scheduled a discovery call to talk about a (VERY expensive) program I was considering investing in. Part of me already knew I was going to sign up before the call even began. To be honest, I was curious how the sales team handled discovery calls for premium programs like this one. This was a GROUP program that cost as much as my 1:1 program did at the time. Even people at my level have things to learn!

While on the phone with the sales representative, I talked about my business, my vision and what was stopping me (nothing at the time). Then he asked me what my monthly financial goal was.

YOUR FIRST SIX FIGURES

"Fifty thousand."

That would be about $600,000 per year—a perfect stretch for me. He fired back with, "What about a hundred thousand dollars a month?"

A huge smile spread across my face.

"Is that even possible? COULD that be possible?"

By my calculations, that meant I would have to help a LOT of people every single month.

Still, I was intrigued. I let him keep going—and he sold me on *his* dream of making $100K a month, replacing my perfectly fine goal of $50K a month.

Needless to say, I signed up for the group program. I adjusted all of my monthly goals to reflect this new vision of $100,000 a month.

But after I sat on it for a few days, I started to feel uneasy. That $100K per month felt just out of reach.

So I decided to stick with my gut—with what felt realistic, what felt doable. To shoot for consistently earning $50K a month was no cop-out. That goal still stretched me, but I knew I wouldn't end up killing myself, burning out or going broke.

So as you set your income goals, I want you to do what I did. Stretch yourself, but be realistic. Yes, 5-figure months and 6-figure launches are all the rage right now, but I'm here to tell you that they're not for everyone.

Three months after that discovery call, I did book $100,000 worth of business in a single month. But it was my decision, not some sales guy's.

YOUR NEW OPERATING SYSTEM

For most coaches and consultants in the niches I work in, you only need to close one or two new clients a month to replace the average 9 to 5 job. If you've only earned $3K to $4K per month through traditional employment, then aim for $5K to $7K. Normalize that new level of income, and you'll soon notice how EVERYTHING in your business just aligns to make that happen.

Then once you've hit that goal, move up to the next one. As you journey to higher and higher limits, watch out for common sabotages like busyness that isn't associated with growing your business, comparing yourself to others, coming down with "Shiny Object Syndrome," or constantly procrastinating until things are perfect. Busy doesn't pay the bills.

It's a fact a new Operating System takes time to get used to. You may have just set a new monthly income goal a few seconds ago but now your palms are getting clammy.

"Can I really do it? Am I just fooling myself? Do I really have what it takes?"

Self-doubt is normal. But it doesn't have to last—not if you use my secret weapon. I touched on it briefly at the beginning of this chapter, but it really deserves a whole page to itself.

My secret weapon? Commitment. Specifically, commitment to a new reality.

If you're used to playing small or even playing medium, then this is going to be a challenge for you. Committing to a new reality before it's actually manifested is the scariest and most profound mindset work you can do. Seeing yourself as the leader and acting from that mindset will completely shift your ability to be paid for who you are.

What does radical commitment look like in everyday life?

Like this:

Commit to revising your daily schedule so that you are ONLY doing what you are here to do, you are standing for what you believe in. And with each passing week, you are closer and closer to cruising past your old income limits.

It's fairly simple, but it does require you deciding what you want and making it non-negotiable.

Black and white. Yes or no. True or false.

Your old mindset versus your new mindset—that is how different they should be. If you're running a new Operating System, learn how to use the damn thing! Don't uninstall it then reinstall the previous version over and over.

Yes, commitment is all or nothing, but it doesn't always look that extreme. For example, a combination of journaling and gratitude has helped me commit to a new reality before it actually manifested (which it did eventually).

Each and every day without fail, I write out my entire life vision—including my answers to the questions "What am I here for?" and "What do I stand for?"

I write in the present tense as if I already have everything I desire, then I write it again in the past tense as if it's already happened.

YOUR NEW OPERATING SYSTEM

An easy place to start with this kind of daily practice is to ask yourself, "What is amazing about my life right now?" Look at what you do have—house, car, family, clients, money in the bank, fans and followers—and celebrate each one of them.

As you write what comes to mind, you realize that what you're grateful for now, you haven't always had. What brings you joy now was once a "new reality" you hadn't manifested yet.

That's why I also give thanks for things that I don't have…YET. It's a great way to future pace since you are already in high vibrations from your gratitude practice. The best part is, your brain doesn't recognize the difference between what you have now and what you don't have yet.

The most important aspect of gratitude journaling is having total clarity on who you are and what you want. Be clear on what you want to happen and how you want it to feel—from business and finances to relationships and your body to opportunities and feelings.

Declare in your journal, "THIS is my new normal. It's normal for me to _____. I am a _____ who _____ ever since _____."

In those spaces, describe the new reality that your new Operating System will manifest. What do you to feel normal one day? What type of person do you have to be to get there? What made the difference in your life and business?

Your mindset is your reality—the one you experience now and the one you want in the future.

Your commitment to a new Operating System

is going to take you places—BIG places. If you told me when I started my entrepreneurial journey that I would own a 7-figure business, reach bestselling author status and have appearances in every major business publication on the planet within the first four years, I don't know if I would have believed you.

It took a lot for me to go from "I hope I can earn forty thousand this year," to "I just reached one million in sales and it's only November."

One of the most important parts of that Operating System update had nothing to do with money or business model.

Remember, your mindset defines what you *do*, as in—what you do for you and also what you do for others.

Because I'm an introvert who barely tolerates human interactions that overstay their welcome, I had no idea taking a stand in my business would require me to be a leader in my industry.

But it did. **Mindset wasn't enough. I had to commit to being a leader.**

So do you.

I wanted to be an exception to the 90% Rule—9 out of every 10 online businesses fails in the first 4 months—and I believe you do, too.

One of my favorite things to tell new *Captivate* students is that becoming one of those 10% doesn't happen overnight. Most businesses that DO make it take 5-7 years to turn a profit. If you can profit with your online business in 2 years, is that not incredible? These facts should sober you up out of any fantasy you have been sold about easy launches and instant money. So while everyone else is buying the lie, trying to make money online (and failing miserably), you can be one of the few who stands out from the crowd or wannabes as a leader worth following.

Leaders are bold. So go and explore interesting new things that have nothing to do with business but everything to do with who you are as a person. Go scuba diving or skydiving. Take a trapeze lesson. Do something to get your heart pumping and give yourself a thrill.

Don't just be another bump on the log. If you're fine with blending into the background in your personal life, you'll soon find yourself blending into the background in your industry.

Nobody wants to be the "best kept secret." But people who become leaders are the ones who actually did something about it.

One of my commitments as a leader is to bring the real me to every article, every webinar, every social media post, every course, every coaching call.

Leaders are authentic. So be yourself. Don't worry about trying to impress anyone or compete with anyone but yourself. When you're a phony, people can smell it a mile away!

To date, my #1 viral piece of content is a post I shared on social media where I revealed every doubt, every insecurity and every mistake I made in my early days in business—and how I overcame them all.

Only when you see yourself as not just someone who is making money, but as someone who is a true bonafide leader can you actually step into that role. And that is a decision not for the faint of heart. The REAL Leadership Mastery I teach in *Captivate* challenges even the most experienced entrepreneurs.

Because that is what being a leader looks like— raw, vulnerable, real. When you commit to being authentic, future members of your tribe will know your worth and want to be a part of whatever you're doing.

When you do share success stories (yours or a client's), don't be a jackass. No one likes a jackass. As a leader, you have a responsibility to be kind, to be easy-going, to be relatable.

That's why tens of thousands of people read my emails before anyone else's—they also know I won't fill their inbox with selfish, arrogant, critical or even mean-spirited content that sucks their enthusiasm out of life. Yes, I'm all about Tough Love, but I say and do everything with love. The end goal is to help, to be useful, to make my industry (and ultimately this world) a better place.

When you are living from the heart like this, people will fall in love with you. Your magnetism will be undeniable. When you upgrade to that new Operating System, you discover who you really are. You see the path to reaching your full potential and you attract relationships and opportunities that are in line with your life's purpose.

With every piece of content you put out there and with every new course you launch, you'll see yourself as a role model. Because your fans and fol-lowers already do.

Customers will say, "I respect you! You inspire

me!" by investing in your programs or products with their hard-earned money.

This is the natural result of focusing on the gifts you have to give to the world—and sharing them without pretense.

At this point in Chapter 1, you're probably motivated to take over the world with your message and ideas.

And that's good. Now that you're adopting a new mindset and upgrading to your new Operating System, I need to tell you one more thing before we find an even greater level of freedom through the second of our eight doors:

All I can do is show you where the doors are and give you the keys. It's your responsibility to walk through them and implement everything you learn in this book.

Taking responsibility for yourself and your actions as a business owner will seem extreme to some. When things don't go quite right, you'll be the first to say, "I failed. It was my fault. I can't blame anyone."

I believe there is something empowering about this level of extreme responsibility. When you rely on yourself to pick yourself back up, you trust your judgment more. You make wiser decisions. You choose better investments. Instead of spending $1 to earn $100, you start finding opportunities to spend $1 and make $1,000.

Yes, there may be times where you spend $1 and make $0.10! When that happens, the personal responsibility you've chosen to take over your life will motivate you to catch yourself. When unproductive behaviors of old patterns of thought creep in, you'll have the awareness to shift your mindset back to where it needs to be. Every potential downward spiral, you'll recognize and avoid.

This "catch and switch" process extends to more than just your thoughts. As an entrepreneur, you also need to take responsibility for being held accountable. That means putting yourself in environments where people will support you and challenge you—and getting yourself OUT of environments where people expect you to live according to an old version of your mental Operating System...or worse, theirs!

Because your vibrational frequency affects every aspect of your life and business, you don't want to be around people who doubt you at every turn, who think the entrepreneurial journey isn't worth the risk.

You and I both know it is. Having support on that journey is key. By reading this book, you are connecting with someone who has already been there. You are truly the sum of the 5 people you hang out with the most, and I'm glad to be one of them while you're digging into this book.

Before we discover the big picture of your market in Chapter 2 (and where your business fits into it), I want to give you with one more thought:

Mindset is like a treasure hunt for your business; the deeper you go, the bigger the results.

Keep on digging.

CHAPTER 2

Understand The Big Picture

Once you have clarity on what you're doing, why you're doing it and for whom you're doing it, everything else becomes effortless.

Your first subscriber.

Your first guest post.

Your first launch.

Your first customer.

Every first in your business is a win. And the more wins you create early on, the more momentum you build.

On my journey from earning $5K a month to $50K a month (then blowing that up to reach 7 figure status), I celebrated every win along the way.

Every successful product launch motivated me to go big or go home with the next one, then go bigger on the one after that.

As I scaled my business from a one-woman show and became a "household name" in the online business world, I just knew that more moves in the right direction—*any* move in the right direction—would keep that momentum building.

But there was only one problem with that—a problem I had to wrestle by the jaws until it retreated into submission.

And that problem was the **"What Got Me Here Will Get Me There" Fallacy**.

As I transitioned from 5 figure launches to 6 figure launches, I patted myself on the back.

"Jenn, you are KILLING it out here!" I told myself.

Sure, the hustle of my early days in business that allowed me to claw myself out of tens of thousands of dollars in debt kept the fire of passion burning brightly inside me.

But when one of my mentors challenged me with a cold-water-to-the-face piece of feedback, I realized that **what got me *here*** (where I was), **wouldn't get me *there*** (where I am now).

"If a minimum wage employee can do it, you as the CEO shouldn't."

That CEO was me. And I knew my mentor was right—everything I had been doing to generate wins in my business would keep me at that level.

But my dreams and ambitions are bigger than what I accomplished yesterday.

So I made one of the most difficult changes a business owner can make.

UNDERSTAND THE BIG PICTURE

I pulled back to re-examine *why* I was trying every new online technique and tactic (and to pinpoint which ones worked the most for my business).

That process alone changed EVERYTHING.

So now when one of my clients approaches me to ask, "Now what?" I challenge her to devote the time to get clear on what actually works.

Not what works **generally**, but what works **specifically for THEIR business**.

As you continue to update your new Operating System with the right applications that will transform your business into an unstoppable force, you have to know **WHY you are doing what you are doing**.

Don't just try XYZ tactic because you saw someone in your industry Tweet about it. And don't just throw more money into advertising because you're seeing a surplus this month.

A large part of walking through the second of eight doors of freedom—"The Big Picture"—has to do with **getting clarity**—about the strategies you need to implement, about the products you need to create and about the Tribe of 1000 True Fans who need you.

Here in Chapter 2, I am going to show you how to get the most PROFITABLE kind of clarity there is—**clarity on who your market is and what they want**.

If you want to establish your legacy by doing truly meaningful and inspiring work, you've got to find your people.

YOUR FIRST SIX FIGURES

Your 1000 True Fans.

By the end of this chapter, you will know how to attract and magnetize these people to your brand.

You will know EXACTLY what burning pains they need solved, how much they are willing to pay to solve them, and why you and ONLY you are the one to do that for them.

And how are you going to get there?

Not by guesswork or unguided brainstorming, I can tell you that! My clients come to me because I "take the gloves off" and call it the way I see it.

You deserve nothing less than that too, sister.

That's why I will show you how to use a combination of Surveys and Interviews that will give you the right data you need to effortlessly create programs and services that make your Tribe click "Buy Now" without hesitation.

None of this is theory. Or hypotheticals. The new way to do market research has already proven itself in my own business and that of dozens of my clients.

Remember what I said earlier about the "What Got Me Here Will Get Me There" Fallacy?

By asking the right questions to my market (and asking them the right way), I got the clarity I needed to create the product and plan the launch that pushed me over the 7 figure mark for the first time.

I got from "here" to "there".

UNDERSTAND THE BIG PICTURE

Let's get you that same kind of clarity too.

It will take work.

But I **promise** you—it will be worth it.

On the other side, any feelings of self-doubt, confusion and overwhelm you've had will be a thing of the past.

So let's cut the bullshit, find your people, nurture the hell out of them and get you paid to be yourself.

#InspiredMuch?

Your new mindset—your new Operating System—is more than just how you think about yourself and your business, it's about WHAT you think about.

I didn't admit this in the last chapter, so I will do it now.

"Mindset" has become a buzzword in online business circles, and its usual definition annoys me. People think that if you just "think" about what you want, you can get it.

Mindset is a process, one that has to be led by those who already have it in them to succeed.

Your new OS is where it all really starts. It doesn't start with tactics or sales scripts or funnels.

You need to get your mind right before you can actually make an impact as a leader. You have to put your ego aside and realize that this NOT about YOU. It's about the people you were put here to serve.

This is why it's critical to have a bigger vision for what you are doing. You have to have...**The Big Picture**.

So, let's turn our full attention to the Tribe you will build—and how they will fall head over high-heels in love with you and your mission.

You want them to feel like you "get them" more than anyone else in your industry. My methods of market research will do just that for you.

Let's dig in then, starting with **a new way to survey your target market**.

In order to create the right programs and services that are effortless for you to create and a no-brainer for your clients to buy, you need the right data.

You need to know what to ask, how to ask it and what to do with the results so you can create a demand before you even offer anything.

To kickoff this survey process, I want you to target 10 people—they could be current clients, people in a Facebook group where your ideal buyers hang out or your email subscribers.

Because I'm a firm believer in the power of Standard Operating Procedures to accelerate that growth of your business, I'm going to give you a short script of questions for your surveys and interviews that you can use every single time you brainstorm a new product, program or service.

You'll need a free survey software, and you'll need to know why someone would be willing to help you out. What's in it for them?

When you know to ask the right questions, you'll get the right answers—questions like, "What are you struggling with most?", "How would it feel to finally have a solution?" and "What have you tried so far?"

UNDERSTAND THE BIG PICTURE

And if you are surveying and interviewing current clients or program members, ask additional questions to really dig deep into why they hired YOU—as opposed to hiring someone else, doing it themselves or ignoring the problem altogether.

These surveys and interviews are critical to understanding The Big Picture of your business. We can't just come up with an idea that seems fun to us, then try to launch a business out of it. That's a hobby.

You're here to create profitable products, programs and services that impact thousands of people. In other words, we cannot afford to NOT do market research first.

Once you catalogue your survey responses, it's time to go beyond your current network. The power of the internet allows us to work with people on other continents and from other cultures. That means our job is to research our target market much more broadly than those first 10 people.

Here's how we're going to do that—my secret weapon of market research.

The internet.

Okay, maybe you saw that one coming!

Websites where people can pour out their thoughts and feelings about other businesses, products and ideas in your industry are totally overlooked by most college-level marketing classes.

Yet real people's real feedback is the key that unlocks our second freedom door. So, why wouldn't we get as much of it as possible?

YOUR FIRST SIX FIGURES

The easiest places to expand your market research activities are Reddit, Quora, Facebook groups, relevant forums, comments on blogs in your industry and Amazon book reviews.

For most of those sites, all you will need to do is search terms like "help with _____" (problem you solve) and "how to _____" (solve their problem).

For Amazon book reviews, the process is more nuanced.

Like the blog comments and Quora questions you'll sort through to find golden nuggets of insight from your target market, you'll be reviewing...reviews!

Type your product idea, primary service or business' niche in the Amazon.com search box. For example, if you create personal branding courses and offer 1:1 coaching, search for "personal branding".

If very few books show up in the search results, that is a red flag your idea may not have enough demand to be worthy of building a business around.

When you do see books appear in the search results, skip over those that have mostly 5-star reviews. Instead, look for books on your topic with only 70-80% 5-star reviews (or fewer).

Because you want real feedback from real people who were willing to pay to solve a problem or fulfill a need, hone in on Verified Reviews that are 4-star, 3-star and 2-star. Most of the extremely positive reviews are from biased friends and family while most of the extremely negative reviews are just haters with a poor command of the English language—"this book suked i hated it don't waste you're mooney."

When you dig into the real reviews, look for what readers did NOT like about the content. What was missing? Were there topics they bought the book for, hoping the author covered them but didn't? What sections or ideas meant the most to them? Were there any strategies or tactics that came off as unrealistic or impractical? Did the author fall into the negative stereotypes of your industry?

Lastly, look for the section "Others also bought" on the page. This will tell you what other problems or needs your market may have that you'll want to include in your product or program.

For the personal branding example, Amazon. com readers are also buying books on networking, sales and marketing.

It's fair to say that, at this point, you will have a LOT of data on your hands...and on your computer.

How can you organize all of it? One word: **buckets**.

In a spreadsheet or blank document, create question-based sections for which you will copy-and-paste all of your market research data into.

This will help you narrow down your target market generally...to your ideal clients specifically.

Questions that you absolutely MUST find the answers to in your research include:

- What does your target market struggle with most as it pertains to what you do?
- What things have they tried before to solve this problem?
- What do they love about the solutions available to them?
- What do they hate about the solutions currently available to them?
- Where is there a gap in the market?
- Who are your top three "competitors"?
- What business models are they working in?
- Who else is your ideal client buying from?
- What books do they read?
- What websites/blogs do they visit daily?
- What social media are they on regularly?
- Do they have money to invest in what you offer?

Yes, these are a lot of questions to answer! But you don't have to answer every single one of them all at once.

If you commit to surveying or interviewing 3 new people per week, that's 12 new people who will learn about you and your business every single month.

Now, if you REALLY want to get crazy, make it your goal to survey or interview 3 new people per DAY. If you follow this challenge for an entire year, then 1,092 new people will have learned about the magic of your work!

Of course, building a profitable business with products and services that sell themselves is more than understanding what your ideal clients and customers are willing to pay for.

The Big Picture is like a Venn diagram—in one of the two circles, you have "everything my target market is willing to pay for". In the other circle, you have "everything I want my business to be about".

Where those two circles overlap—that is where you and your business belong. That is the space from which you can build a limitless legacy. You are offering your greatest gifts to the world that they need the most...and they're willing to pay hand-somely for them.

When you know what you want your legacy to be, you're able to take lots of aligned action. It's like an exercise—you're strengthening the muscles of your business.

When you what all The Big Picture includes, you have the rock-solid confidence to take calculated risks, deepen the trust within yourself and create opportunities that lead to a prosperous future.

So, yes, you absolutely need to get that clarity on your ideal clients.

But you also need clarity on your ideal BUSINESS.

What does your ideal day look like, from when you kick off the covers in the morning to when you close that laptop at the end of the day's working hours?

Who is on your dream team? Virtual Assistants, Community Managers, Copywriters, Graphic De-signers, Coaches?

How do you want to feel when you're working hard? Yes, it takes hard work to sustain growth, but you don't have to straddle the edge of burnout everyday.

Who are your customers? What do they love about your brand, your products? When they tell their friends to sign up for your services or join whatever you launch next, what do they say?

Each of your answers to these is important. But collectively, they form a picture SO big that you will NEVER deviate from the right path when it comes to building your business.

So, let's combine what you've learned about your ideal clients with what you imagine your ideal business looks like.

Write your **Big Picture Declaration**. Use the outline below as inspiration to fill in the blanks with your answers:

I _____ , will create a business that allows me to _____ , _____and _____.

I'm doing this because_____ _____ .

I work with_____ (target market) to help them_____ _____by _____ (your process).

I am uniquely suited to serve my clients because _____ _____ _____ .

I work with people who are_____ , _____ and _____.

UNDERSTAND THE BIG PICTURE

With my help, they are able to _____
_____. Without my help,
they will _____
_____ .

I earn $_____ per year
through my work. This money allows me to
_____
_____ .

I am _____ (adjec-
tive that describes you) and I am the best damn
_____ (title/occupation)
there is.

Once you write all of that down, print it off!
Turn your favorite phrases into images you can
make your wallpaper on your computer, tablet and
phone. Stand on who you are, and stand up for the
people who need you most!

What we're really working toward here is what
I call your "**Zone of Genius**". If your Big Picture
Declaration is about you, your business and your
target market, your Zone of Genius is about the
EXPERIENCE people enjoy through your products
and services.

Your Zone of Genius is the answer to the question, "What do people get from you that they just
cannot get anywhere else?"

That doesn't mean you have to reinvent the
wheel. You are brilliant at things that other people
have no idea how to do—but wish they could.

So, what are people always coming to you for?
What can you do that seems SO easy for you, but
others seem to struggle with? What can you do with
your eyes closed and hands tied behind your back?

Your business is about more than just you. It's about giving people an experience worthy of their time, their effort, their money.

And in turn, they will reward you with the income, lifestyle and impact you might not even be able to imagine yet.

But all of that requires you to recognize where your Zone of Genius is, and do everything you can to make that your business' focus from here on out.

That's why I like this quote from motivational speaker Les Brown:

"The graveyard is the richest place on earth, because it is here that you will find all the hopes and dreams that were never fulfilled."

All those Zones of Genius unoccupied, all those people who needed them but they weren't there.

I refuse to make that mistake. And I know that by purchasing this book and following every step I lay out for you, you refuse to make that mistake, too.

However, a Zone of Genius is just an idea without the right business model.

One of the top causes of entrepreneur burnout is using business models that are not customized to your particular vision, personality, strengths and weaknesses.

Why wouldn't it be? If you borrow a business model from someone else in your industry, you might as well just stay in your 9-5! The whole point of entrepreneurship is to do it YOUR way. No two graduates of *Captivate* have the same business model, for example. Even if they're in the exact same industry and offer similar services!

It's critical to use a business model that is based on you feeling good about yourself, and your customers feeling good about doing business with you, rather than keeping you in a cycle of scarcity and deprivation where you're always trying to "make things happen".

To close out this chapter, I want to give your Big Picture Declaration a route to become your Big Reality and your Zone of Genius to become a practical business model that entices all the right people.

By identifying the right business model for you, you'll be able to scale your business in ways that are designed to accelerate your growth while minimize growing pains.

Choosing to create a business that is sustainable is as much about your ability to be resilient as it is being strategic—you need both.

Big Picture Declarations are collective goals, not prayers that some way somehow, you'll be successful someday.

Most people want to scale to quickly, but you can't scale until you have a proven model to do so. Your business will thrive and can 2X, 3X or 10X based on you doing what feels good and what allows you to shine. Because those are different for everyone, let's review the Pros and Cons of the most popular business models today.

With the **1:1 Coaching** business model, you get to learn a lot about your ideal clients, work with them intimately, charge higher fees and customize your work for each client (Pros).

But you're still trading hours for dollars, and the model of 1:1 work isn't scalable (Cons).

With the **Group Coaching** business model, you can work one to many, leverage your time and create a community of accountability that helps drive results (Pros).

But you have to know your ideal client well enough to create a solution that can be delivered in a group setting (Con).

With the **Consultant** business model, you can charge higher fees and tell clients exactly what to do in order to create a small army of success stories (Pros).

But you must have proven experience offering that service, or else no one will believe you're credible (Cons).

With the **Done For You** business model, there is no 1:1 work, which is ideal for independent works (Pros).

But you and your team must do all the work, which could be labor and time intensive. Even then, some clients may not like or agree with the finished product (Cons).

With the **Course Publisher** business model, there is no 1:1 work, you can serve a lot more people at one time, you can spread your message further to much more people and ultimately have a bigger impact on the planet (Pros).

But this model requires a LOT of content, the ability to reach an enormous amount of new people constantly, and much lower price points (Cons).

With the **Membership Site** business model, you're earning recurring monthly revenue. Plus, it's scalable. Entrepreneurs with a flair for content creation tend to fall in love with it and never look back (Pros).

But you must have community that trusts you, a lot of initial set up is required, there will be constant turnover and it's your job to create more and more content to keep members happy with their subscription over the long haul (Cons).

With the **Speaker/Workshop** business model, you can build authority, get paid high fees and book new clients while selling from the stage (Pros).

But this Solopreneur business model requires you to have rock star credibility, travel often and put in the time to build and maintain your reputation (Cons).

At this point, the wheels are turning so fast inside your mind you might be worried about flying off track.

So take a moment. Pause. Breathe.

My explanation of each business model is intended to help you pick ONE.

Just one.

Which model affords you the longevity, scalability and freedom that your Big Picture Declaration describes? Which model allows you to incorporate your Zone of Genius in the most effective and feel-good way?

Pick one.

We don't need to become serial entrepreneurs quite yet! Because at the very beginning of Chapter 3, we are going to apply your business model of choice to getting you the most exciting result yet:

As much money as quickly as possible with the least amount of effort.

You game?

CHAPTER 3

Your Profit Potential

If you're not making money and you're not making sales, you don't have a business. You have a really expensive hobby.

I've learned a couple of things about human nature since starting my business a few years ago.

One, we can get INSANELY jealous of other people who look like they're succeeding effortlessly at something that makes us pound our foreheads into the keyboard.

Two, what usually LOOKS like effortless success is never effortless. Behind the scenes, some sister is her working her ass off to make shit happen, hustle for as many customers as she can find and seize every opportunity she gets.

Both of these things come up with one of the most sensitive topics of conversation today—**money**.

Revenue.

Profit.

Income.

For entrepreneurs like me whose income is now a factor of 20 times higher than what I made in the 9-to-5 world, we know what it takes to achieve so-called "effortless" success.

That's why I just tune people out who think they can excuse away other people's success because they haven't done their due diligence to achieve that success themselves.

So, when I DO talk about my business' profit margins and the income I get to enjoy because of them, it's NEVER to show off.

That's the first thing I want to get across to you as we charge through the third door of freedom, "Your Profit Potential":

Look at the success of others as an example for you to follow and as inspiration that yes, you CAN achieve what you desire.

I was in a ton of debt. I was stuck in a toxic relationship (several, actually). I had a business that gave me a NEGATIVE income at one time.

So I've been there, and I get it.

To achieve your financial goals, it's not about putting in more hours or sacrificing time to rejuvenate yourself. That vicious cycle will kill your motivation faster than reading all of those "I made $1 million in 2 weeks working 1 hour a day" articles floating around on social media.

To realize your profit potential, you have to follow a series of proven steps that—by following those steps—give you the best possible chance of "making it" in business.

I've walked that walk. And so have my clients. This year alone, I've helped entrepreneurs:

- **Achieve $80,000+ product launches**
- **Earn $30,000 in 1 month**
- **Book 3 new clients within 1 week of starting work together**
- **See their very first 5-figure months—and keep that consistent**
- **Finally reach 6-figures in revenue**
- **Quit their 6-figure corporate jobs**
- **Sell out group programs weeks in advance**

For all of these clients—and now for *you*—I consider myself a **business partner in crime**. Your accomplishments keep me in business. So earning the income I do now isn't about me (or about making others feel jealous), it's about showing as many people as possible how to walk through the same doorway to freedom that I have.

By the end of this chapter, I want you to have a newfound true belief in yourself, your business and your ability to exponentially increase your earning potential.

And most importantly, by the end of this chapter, you will know how to start building cash flow by just being yourself! How awesome is that?

Now, there will be a few tricky areas that require tighter navigation, like pricing and cash injection, but the course I have charted for you is the safest there is.

YOUR FIRST SIX FIGURES

As we start this journey toward profitability together, we have some questions to answer.

Like you learned in Chapter 2, owning a revenue-churning business you can depend on for decades to come isn't JUST about what you want to offer—you have to do your research first (and if you applied what you learned in Chapter 2, you already have).

In other words, find the "sweet spot" where the needs of your ideal client and your expertise, knowledge and skills overlap.

That is Business Viability 101. If your idea for a product, brand or service has no prospects out there waiting for a solution like yours that hasn't been created yet...what does that tell you? (And vice-versa.)

Take a look and see if people are willing to buy what you plan to offer or sell. Are people buying (LOTS of) books on Amazon related to your niche? Are there currently other service providers who offer 1:1 Coaching or Done For You similar to what you want to offer? Are businesses paying for ads on Facebook, Instagram or Google to market products and programs in your industry?

All of those are strong indicators that YES, you are in the right place at the right time to start and grow a profitable business in your chosen niche.

Be careful about sheer numbers though. I see SO many online businesses that attract massive audiences and grow lists of hundreds of thousands of subscribers...yet the owners barely make $500 a month!

WTF, right?

It's because they focus on free above everything else.

Free ebooks. Free webinars. Free trainings. Free discovery calls.

Over time, these entrepreneurs taught their Tribes that their knowledge and experience was NOT worth paying for—and so they never did.

Ouch...

I've said it a thousand time before, and I'll say it again:

Online businesses thrive by having a list of subscribers who BUY, not a list of subscribers who... well...*subscribed.*

Once you have decided that your business is an actual business—and not a Freebie Factory—there's something else to consider about your future buyers.

And that is, what else have they already bought? And WHO have they bought from?

Yes, we're getting into competitive analysis mode here. But this is especially important if you are entering an overly crowded field like Life Coaching or a field with longevity like Digital Marketing.

YOUR FIRST SIX FIGURES

When it comes to your competition, there's really only one question you need to answer: **WHY does your target market buy from them?**

The answers to that will tell you everything you need to know about where you fit in your future customers' world.

Does your competition already create high quality products and offer excellent services, but perhaps they're too broad?

Does your competition just happen to use the right keywords in their content marketing, so they get picked first—and not because they're the best?

At the end of the day (or rather, at the beginning—we don't want to wait THAT long), if you're in an industry with ZERO competition, that tells you two fortunate truths.

One, there isn't a need for it.

Two, people aren't willing to pay for it.

Yes, the word "fortunate" there was intentional. Rather than waste years of your life pounding the so-called pavement pitching products no one wants, you can focus your efforts on a niche that has already proven profitable.

This one lesson alone has earned me more Thank You notes from more people than I have time to respond to.

Seriously. If you don't have any competition, you have no available customers.

But when you DO find real competitors, it's your job to dig deeper into your ideal client's world better than they have.

What can you offer better, faster or cheaper?

If you're a web developer, can you build an easier-to-use website in half the time?

If you're a copywriter, can you write more emotionally rich copy for product launch funnels that convert 25% more subscribers into buyers?

If you're a business coach, can you empower your clients to shift their worldview and achieve transformational results without time-consuming homework that other coaches require?

Whatever your industry, put yourself ahead of the game.

Give your ideal clients a reason to view your business as ideal for them, too.

And once you've won their business once, don't stop there—PLEASE don't stop there.

You want your business to produce an income for you and your family that lasts a lifetime and beyond, right?

Then build a business that offers customers *lifetime value*.

According to the White House Office of Consumer Affairs, it is 6 to 7 times MORE expensive to acquire a new customer than to turn a past one into a repeat buyer.

Let's flip that statistic for a second. Most entre-preneurs I meet on the web or in person focus on launching that one HUGE program or enrolling a TON of clients for their flagship service.

It's a focus on getting MORE people, ALL the time into their Tribe. To that, I ask...

Why?

If you spend your marketing, promotion and advertising efforts on turning a one-off buyer into a two-time, three-time, ten-time buyer, then you are SLASHING your acquisition costs by a factor of 6-7X.

A stat like that gets through to most people. But then there's a bigger problem...

How?

Let's say you have a program that you launch once a quarter, or maybe you're running an ever-green funnel.

Now, pick apart your own program. What's missing?

What could you have included if you had an extra 30-60 days to create new content?

And what have you learned about your customers' needs from people who HAVE gone through your program?

Brainstorm answers to questions like these, and those are your cross-sell and upsell programs!

Opportunities for repeat business should always come as a value-add though and not just be a re-packaging of what people have already purchased. That's a recipe for bad reviews, unsubscribes and so many refund requests that PayPal might consider closing your account!

Value is a two-way street. Selling a product or service that will be useful to the same customer years down the road means that your profit potential will remain steady.

Without that consistency, it is VERY hard to maintain the growth of a business. That's why I have nearly a DOZEN different programs, including *The Little Black Business Book*, *Captivate*, *Continuity Rocks*, *Get Paid To Be You*, *Five Figure Funnels*, *Gutsy Girls Make Green* and *Get P.A.I.D.*

Multiple streams of income are the lifeblood of 7-figure businesses like mine that see explosive growth month after month, year after year.

If you only have one or two ways for people to work with you, you are leaving many, MANY opportunities for people to say NO. The days I struggled the most in my business were the days I offered only 1:1 Coaching and Membership Site products.

Whether you're on offer #2 or product #20, another excellent way to increase your profits is to spend more of them.

Yes, you read that right.

Specifically, spend more of your profits on *outsourcing*.

Consider this:

If it takes you 80 hours to launch a Membership Site, but only 15-20 hours of that total goes to content creation, then why are you spending that extra 60-65 hours on designing graphics, editing videos and audios and uploading content to the Site?

Hire a Virtual Assistant who specializes in ecommerce. Ask around in the Facebook groups for entrepreneurs that you frequent, and you'll have at least a half-dozen recommendations for VA's to interview.

Then, devote those now freed-up 60-65 hours to setting up affiliate agreements, writing guest posts and scheduling Facebook ads—all in a concerted effort to sell out every membership spot you have.

When it comes down to the numbers, you'll spend a few hundred dollars to make an extra several THOUSAND dollars.

Smart move, sister.

But Membership Sites may not be for everyone—I get it. There are aspiring entrepreneurs reading this book who cannot fathom investing another 15-20 hours into product development with no promises of profit after a launch.

So for people reading this who have a hankering for the low-hanging fruit of online business—you just want to bring some quick cash into the business ASAP—there's a solution for you, too.

YOUR PROFIT POTENTIAL

It's a 2-step solution. Easy. Simple.

You're going to leverage the connections you have now and turn them into pure profit.

First, make a list of people you've spoken to about your business...but they did NOT become clients.

Second, make another list of people you've connected with online...that COULD be potential clients.

For both lists of people, you're going to send them a personalized message that begins with 6 precious little words:

"Do you still need help with _____ ?"

For each recipient, you'll mention the service they expressed interest in or the problem they told you they have.

As long as the problem is an urgent one that you can solve with your product or service, expect a solid response.

Even if you aim for a conservative 2-3% conversion rate, for every 100 people you email that 1 sentence to, you can expect about 2-3 new clients.

Do the math on that, and the low-hanging fruit becomes a feast VERY quickly.

As desperation for cash flow turns into confidence in your viable business, you will start to notice something. (This is also true for entrepreneurs who see consistent 4-figure months and want to reach 5-figures, or they see 5-figures and plan to achieve 6-figures per month.)

YOUR FIRST SIX FIGURES

This something is **the problem of pricing**, AKA how much you should charge for your products and services.

It's fairly common practice to increase your profits by increasing your prices. But how exactly do you do that without pissing off customers who then decide to go elsewhere?

Regardless of what your pricing eventually looks like, you want people to truly see the value in your work. You want to align with prices that are driven by your results rather than the nebulous "what people will pay".

A couple of years ago, I realized it was time to increase my rates when I had as many testimonials and success stories coming from my FREE content as my paid courses and coaching!

That was my wake-up call—my stuff is DAMN valuable, and people should pay for it.

ALL of it.

My motto had been, "You can never give too much for free," but it was clear that I let people take advantage of me.

Being a giver who loves to serve others is NEVER a good excuse to let that happen.

So, I fired clients who wanted hand-holding and codependent relationships with their business coach.

I decided to work ONLY with go-getters and industry leaders-in-the-making who were willing to do what it takes—including *invest* in what it takes—to make their dreams a reality.

Never again was I going to accept a $1,000 check for helping someone earn $100,000.

And you shouldn't either.

Even if your industry is "soft skills" or doesn't involve calculations for direct Return-On-Investment, there are still ways to justify higher prices.

But "higher" is arbitrary. Let's look at a sliding scale to determine where you are now, versus where you want to be.

This sliding scale has 3 types of rates: Fuck This, Feel Good and Fantastic.

So, where does your current rate fall?

Do you put in hours of effort, sacrificing time with family, only to end up holding a grudge because the prospect DID become a client?

Then you're charging Fuck This prices.

Do you never see a single complaint about the price of products you launch, or do prospects become clients without even a hint of negotiation required?

Then you're charging Feel Good prices.

But do you WANT a filter that prevents so-so customers and pain-in-the-ass clients from ever attempting to do business with you?

Then you need to charge Fantastic prices.

YOUR FIRST SIX FIGURES

Only when you start to feel a pushback from the type of clients and customers you would rather NOT work with will you know your rates are starting to be in the right area of the scale.

If your target market isn't willing to pay for results, they don't deserve them—that may seem like a harsh statement, but you're running a business, not a charity. I'm all for donations of time and money to stellar causes, but entrepreneurs are better off not mixing the two. Then nobody wins.

Lowering your rates lowers your ideal clients' respect for you—it's as simple as that.

With that said, you're now ready to do the opposite—raise those rates and earn that respect.

You know where your Fantastic rates are, and you want people to pay them.

For current customers who purchased one of your programs, or for current clients who are on a contract, the advice you're about to take does not apply. That means for any other case, it DOES.

To every customer in a month-to-month membership program and to current clients that you bill per hour or per project, send them a quick message highlighting some of the recent results they and others have achieved by working with you.

Be sure to focus on specific numbers if you can! Then, write something like:

"Because of the massive results I've been able to get for my clients, my roster is filling up fast

and my rates will be increasing as a result. My current rates will be increasing from $_____ to $_____ as of _____ date."

When my own clients use a script like this, the pricing increase ALWAYS pays for any drop-offs that occur...and then some.

Wouldn't you rather weed out the people who don't think you're worth it? I did—and it was one of the most freeing things I've ever done in my life, aside from *starting* my business in the first place.

That's the power of knowing and staying true to Your Profit Potential.

At the beginning of this chapter, I told you that effortless success is never really effortless.

Just raising your rates by 10% once a year without doing anything else to increase cash flow is not going to have the transformative effect some might hope for.

This business thing takes work. It takes focus. And it takes hustle.

Notice what I didn't say there—*talent*. Because hustle ALWAYS beats talent when talent doesn't hustle.

But there's a word to the wise that comes as a companion to that statement:

"Hustling" is not the same thing as "forever teetering on the edge of burnout."

Your business is only as strong as you are. Just as you need to stand on your value and charge according to that value, you need to stand up for yourself and your sanity.

Manage your energy, protect your boundaries and arrange your schedule according to YOUR priorities, not anyone else's.

Even today, whenever a potential client requests a time on my calendar that I have reserved for time with my son, guess what? She either has to pick another time, or she doesn't have the privilege of becoming a client.

When you know your priorities, everything is black and white like that.

For many entrepreneurs I meet, however, all they see is gray. They cannot always tell where time and energy are well-spent or where they aren't.

"Is that task taking too long? Should I outsource it? Or am I better off biting the bullet and just getting it done? What can I cut out to free up more creative time?"

Those are questions I cannot answer for you. Only two things can—your priorities and your schedule.

If family is a priority, then you know it. Period.

But for most of clients, their real-life schedule is very telling as well.

By real-life schedule I mean, what you ACTU-ALLY spend your time doing—not what you WISH you spent your time doing.

So for the next week, track your daily activities. But don't write a To-Do List, write a To-Done List. Don't track what you *want* to do, track what you actually *did*.

YOUR PROFIT POTENTIAL

Spent 45 minutes trying to edit a snippet of code for your website that a web developer from Fiverr.com could have fixed in 30 seconds for $5? Write it down.

Pretty quickly, you'll realize which tasks lead directly to profit and which suck the sanity out of your soul.

Then, ruthlessly cut out of your schedule anything and everything that doesn't align with your family and financial priorities. Delegate. Outsource. Subcontract. Whatever it takes.

No, the end of this chapter is not exactly tactical. There is no Step 1, Step 2, Step 3.

That is where mindset comes in.

A few months ago, I had a call for a potential interview on Yahoo.com. The interviewer asked me about my ideas for her working title piece, "The 5 Biggest Mistakes Entrepreneurs Make".
When I told her about the patterns I see consistently in clients who come to me, she didn't get it.

I talked about mindset, belief and confidence, but she wanted more practical things—like adding an opt-in box and social media buttons to a website.

Ummm... no. None of that matters without the strong foundation. To be a successful entrepreneur, you need more than tips and tricks.

And to reach Your Profit Potential, you need more than homework to complete—you need to understand why your clients value you, stand on that value as firmly as you can and eliminate every task and operation in your business from your plate that doesn't align with you creating more of that value-worth-paying-top-dollar-for.

Because if you overexert yourself by hustling in areas that don't move you closer to your true priorities, you will kill your passion.

That is not what I want for you.

The third door is open—will you walk through it with me?

CHAPTER 4

Simple Social Influence

Make them fall in love with your soul, and they will open up their wallets.

Influence.

It's the topic of bestselling books.

Thousands of articles a WEEK are written about it.

Millions of aspiring entrepreneurs claim they want it.

So... What exactly is influence? And how is it the fourth of our eight doors to freedom?

Rather than a jargon-laced definition of influence, I'll tell you what influence looks like in the real world of the online entrepreneur.

Influence is your ability to inspire others to see the world the way you do and to motivate them to take action according to that worldview.

The truth is clear—you either have influence, or you don't.

People read your blog posts or they don't. They subscribe to your list or they don't. They buy your programs or they don't.

And they believe you're a trustworthy expert or they don't.

THAT is a bitter pill to take for many aspiring entrepreneurs I meet. They think all they have to do to "make it" and sell 100 course licenses a month for $1,000 each is throw up an opt-in, scribble a few ideas for emails, nab a free sales page template and they're set!

<Insert Skipping Record Sound Effect>

To quote the infamous meme...

"That's not how it works. That's not how any of this works!"

Influence isn't created in an afternoon of brainstorming or journaling.

Influence ONLY exists when you connect with thousands of people and build a dedicated subscriber list of true fans and followers.

THAT is when you can affect the way people think, feel and act.

Fortunately, you have social media at your disposal to make that your reality, and I'm devoting this chapter to making it as SIMPLE as possible.

You with me?

Get ready to dig deep into the real YOU— I call this "Leveraging Your Backstory" in *Captivate*—and you will naturally remain "top of mind" in your audience's feeds. As the content you create goes viral, you get to enjoy a steady flow of clientele who know about you before ever meeting you personally.

To summarize, **you are going to unleash the leader within.**

Like influence—which you cannot fake—the first step to unleash your inner leader is to position yourself as having expert status.

People know an expert when they see one.

And they can tell when someone isn't the real deal.

Fortunately, positioning yourself as THE expert in your industry or niche is not about having encyclopedia-like knowledge.

Being the expert is about helping others transform their situations—and just as importantly, it's about training others to EXPECT life-transforming results.

The way to do that? **Get them to value your authority.**

THAT is the difference between marketing that attracts and executes versus marketing that is uncompelling and lukewarm.

I see WAY too many entrepreneurs get their authority positioning wrong. They try to be the functional "Jill Of All Trades" type, where they talk about anything and everything under their industry's particular sun in hopes they will reach more people.

Influence doesn't come from being functional like that; influence comes from being VITAL.

Vital to your fans' and followers' success. Vital to your clients' and customers' lives and businesses. Vital to your audience's belief in themselves.

So don't try to be the expert at everything. **Position yourself instead as THE ultimate authority in ONE thing.**

Just one.

YOUR one thing.

The need to focus on only one thing is so critical to influence that it's the title of the 2013 bestseller from Gary Keller, chairman of Keller Williams Realty, Inc: *The ONE Thing*.

I am devoting the beginning of this chapter to solving the problem that comes to many business owners' minds when they read the title of Gary's book:

"But I don't KNOW what my 'one thing' is!"

I'm with you, sister.

And we're going to trail-blaze a path through uncertainty to find your ONE thing.

First, we have to narrow down what you are best at, the areas where you can help your tribe achieve KILLER results in their lives or businesses.

For example, what features are unique about your product or service that no one else offers?

SIMPLE SOCIAL INFLUENCE

When people write or record testimonials for you, what benefits do they describe about working with you that you've NEVER heard about anyone else?

Are certain emotional needs fulfilled by your product or service in a way that no one else can?

Even areas as simple as pricing or branding can help you identify your ONE thing. Do you offer higher quality for a better price than anyone else? Is your brand more exciting, humorous or relevant to your tribe than any of your competitors'?

This gets into your competitive advantage, which basically means that your expertise and authority in your niche is graded on a scale.

In other words, to make your business stand apart from the crowd, all you have to do is be MORE of an expert in your niche than the competition, MORE of an authority on the products or services you offer than your competitors are on theirs.

And then there is the one area that NO ONE can even come close to you on—your unique personality.

What do people enjoy about reading your emails? Why do people share your posts on social media? How do you uniquely draw people in with your quirks, your catchphrases and your outlook on your industry?

Collectively, your answers to these questions are what give you influence.

The way you offer your gifts to the world in ways no one else can—THAT gives you your authority positioning and establishes you as THE expert.

Your ideal clients are drawn to you because of that. Customers are easier to come by. Adoring fans gladly spread the word about what you do because they look at you and think, "She's the one for me!"

On the other hand, if you don't provide customers with a unique experience, offer greater results than your competitors can, present the benefits of your products or services in a clearer way or infuse your personality into your platform, your target market has no good reasons to choose you over the competition.

If that's the case, building an audience will be a chore. Getting customers to pay attention to you will be a constant struggle.

So do yourself a favor; commit to positioning yourself as THE expert for your ideal clients—whatever it takes, no matter your fears or insecurities.

Without it, you have no influence.

But WITH influence, the world is yours. So reach out and grab it!

Because once you get that authority positioning right—the strategy—it's SO much easier to create and share content that pulls people in—the tactics.

You've probably heard is said that entrepreneurs should "be everywhere" online. The usual definition of this is to post constantly on every social network known to humankind.

That's not how I built my 7-figure business, so I won't recommend that to you. Yes, you DO want to be everywhere, but you don't want to be everywhere for EVERYONE.

SIMPLE SOCIAL INFLUENCE

All you need to do to change the status of your online business relationships from Helpful "Friend" to Respected Expert is to broadcast your messages on the channels where your ideal clients hang out the most.

For now, pick TWO social media platforms—not 10 or 20. Whether it's Facebook and Instagram, Twitter and LinkedIn or Periscope and Pinterest, commit to posting at least 2 times each day. Use tools like HootSuite, Buffer or Meet Edgar to manage the scheduling, or just hire a Virtual Assistant and delegate that task.

Remember, if an employee can do it, you as the CEO shouldn't!

Your job is to elevate yourself from the status quo and get seen as someone who is a contender for real impact. That means your primary responsibility as an influencer is to create impactful content.

It doesn't matter if you post on every single social network if no one sees it! That's why you need to stick with just 2 platforms to share that impactful content people look forward to reading, saving and sharing.

For me, being able to come up with aligned content, facing my visibility fears and reaching for a deeper truth is not about reinventing the wheel every single time I put pen to paper (or fingers to keyboard). Visibility is about more than just flooding news feeds; killer content is about more than just showing your face.

That's why I follow the templates that work best when it comes to influencing the masses. And that's what I am going to share with you next—the most powerful post templates that create the most engagement.

Before we dig into *what* to say—the very next section in this chapter—it's important to know *how*. Hence, the templates:

When it comes to social media post templates, **stories** are my #1 favorite. Because stories sell. Period. Stories make you relatable and likable to your audience.

My all-time highest shared post was the story of how I "failed forward" after starting my business. That sort of content allows people to see you as a real person, not just a business owner or a company trying to sell them something.

Stories of wins, struggles and triumphs or overcoming things resonate with people—YOUR people. Use the story post template, and I guarantee you will see an increase in engagement—and influence.

Another template I love is the **ice-breaker**. It's an often overlooked post, but people fucking LOVE it.

For example, one of my few 1:1 Coaching clients is an astrologist. I recommended that she write an ice-breaker post that asked her audience a simple question: "What's your sign?"

The thing exploded with comments and shares for the next WEEK!

Another client is a health coach, and I advised her to ask: "What's your favorite comfort food?"

If you're struggling to get your social media followers engaging with you, the icebreaker post is the fastest way to move people to finally comment and share.

Next is the **positioning questions** template. These questions are a little more in-depth than the ice-breakers. These posts relate directly to your expertise. Do enough of these and people will finally "get it".

For example, as a business coach, I can ask: "What is your biggest struggle when it comes to marketing and visibility?"

Not only do simple questions like that imply to my audience that I'm the one with the answers, they allow me to GIVE the answers people want most. Expertise, demonstrated!

Then there are the easy-peasy **tips and tricks**. Offer a single, memorable tactic to implement ASAP. Step 1, Step 2, Step 3. The more practical, the better.

Despite the anti-math attitudes we see a lot nowadays, people LOVE numbers—I'm talking **results and case studies**.

Numbers of new clients, increases in revenue, pounds shed, inches lost, hours gained—if your clients and customers have those to report, share them!

This goes beyond business and fitness. For example, if you're a life coach, tell the stories of how your clients have found healing from something they've carried with them for 30+ years or how that one single girl you work with finally got a date after 24 months of being single with no hope in sight.

Then there are **memes and quotes**. Pretty simple, right? People love memes, right?

Yes, but you don't want to become Buzzfeed 2.0. Instead of sharing what other people do over and over, use software like Canva or WordSwag to create your own memes and quotes.

Change background colors to match your brand colors, and your images will stand out on social media. Whenever you can give your audience a chuckle with a new take on an old meme, or make them think with a quote from one of your articles, interviews or programs.

What else do people love besides laughing and feeling smart? Giving their **opinions**! Sites like Facebook offer the option to create polls, so you can ask your audience for their perspective on the name of your next webinar, your new opt-in freebie, the next article you should write or even what to call the program you launch next.

Opinion posts give you the added benefit of involving your audience in the creation process, which endears them to you even more.

These social media post templates, like the earlier list of the different social media sites, is not meant to be your to-do list. Better to post daily on 2 sites than hardly ever on 12.

With these posts, plan on writing just 1 per day for the next 30 days. You can start at the beginning of the list of templates, and go through 1 per day, creating a unique piece of content to share and engage your audience.

SIMPLE SOCIAL INFLUENCE

The most important aspect of broadening your social influence is to simply SHOW UP.

Just show up!

If I had a quarter for every new entrepreneur who hasn't even shown up consistently on people's radar, I'd be even richer than I am now.

In order to shine online, you have to be visible to your potential clients. In order to influence them, you've got to show up. Every day. Even when you don't want to.

Show up, do the work, give value, create, coach, create some more, coach some more, invest and keep going, going, going.

Commit to yourself, your business and your clients.

But raw motivation and Jenn Scalia's templates alone won't do it.

Now that you know what *types* of content you've got to work with—the how—let's get strategic about your content marketing—the what.

When you create and share content that is not only meaningful to you but also aligns with the needs, priorities and struggles of your ideal client, everything you write will impact and influence.

Before you sit down and write a story post or create a custom image-based quote, **think deeper about your target market than your competitors do.**

What does your ideal client want? Not just *need*, but WANT?

What are their biggest struggles? How can you solve them?

And most importantly, how can you RELATE to those struggles?

The last thing you want to do is come off as preachy or "holier than thou". That's why you will rarely see me use the word "should," as in, "You should do this, you should do that."

The fact is, if I'm recommending that you do something, I've already tested it in my own business and those of my clients, so you know it's proven.

I believe in authenticity, transparency and real-ness. Walk the walk and talking the talk.

How the hell can I write an epic piece of content that gets shared by the masses if I haven't experienced myself what I'm writing about?

The thing is, our authentic marketing voice can get stifled if we're listening to others too much. I'm all for role models, but it's easy to become an involuntary copycat.

So when you create that valuable content that speaks to your tribe's deepest desires, turn off the noise. Unsubscribe from notifications and newsletters if you have to.

If you're going to influence your audience to take action and do business with you, you've got to play to your strengths and your experience.

No one can fake those.

So do what feels good, and leave the rest to the copycats.

I hereby give your permission to BE YOUR FUCKING SELF.

If you have 2 minutes on a soapbox, what would you say? Turn whatever your answer is into your next story post where you offer a powerful insight into solving your tribe's worst problem.

Whatever you do, whatever you say, whatever you write... DON'T apologize. And don't put fluff out there.

Just say it.

Without a consistent and clear message, your audience will be confused. If you're constantly flip-flopping with your message, if you're inconsistent with what you post and when, people won't trust you. *Looking at you, copycats!*

Don't make the mistake of hiding your true self when you're marketing your content. Being worried about what people will think while trying to be everything to everyone is not just a recipe for disaster, it's the whole fucking buffet of disasters!

So when you do broadcast who you really are and what you're really about to the world, use every weapon of communication you've got—including the one I haven't yet mentioned in this chapter:

Email.

To be on a continuous upward curve of revenue, you have to be in the habit of always collecting new leads.

Fortunately, you can build your email list of leads on a budget.

This is how I built an audience of tens of thousands of women who look forward to seeing my name and face in their inboxes every single day. Email marketing is the oldest, most tried and true method of building a business that lasts.

Email even withstood the Dot-Com Bubble Burst of 2000-2001!

Now that you know how to GIVE your audience the best you have to offer, let's discover how you can GET your audience on that email list in the first place!

A super-engaged email list is the fastest and best way to create a steady flow of clients and customers.

The art and science of list-building is often overlooked by rookie entrepreneurs who get distracted by social media.

While you know that social media is potentially a great way to turn fans into buyers, the most powerful tool to influence your tribe is that email list. Subscribers are your warmest leads and should be nurtured as such.

So how do you grow your list, especially if you're starting from scratch and only have a few followers on social media?

Come with me, we're about to dig into the FIVE ways I've grown my own subscriber list from fewer than a dozen people who barely knew who I was, to tens of THOUSANDS of followers who cannot wait to hear from me.

To grow your audience—and therefore the number of people you can influence—offer a **free webinar**.

Hosting a webinar or teleclass positions you as the expert in your niche. Choose a topic that your target market is struggling with and teach them how to overcome this problem in your webinar.

This is your opportunity to really showcase your expertise and show potential clients that you know what you're talking about. It's also one of the easiest to things to set up and implement, even if you're a new coach. All you need is a lead capture tool such as LeadPages and a computer or smartphone!

Put a **stellar lead magnet** to use as well. A lead magnet, also known as a freebie, freemium or "ethical bribe" is something that you offer your audience in exchange for their email address.

Gone are the days when "Sign up to receive my newsletter!" was enough to get someone to sign up for your list. Your lead magnet gives your audience a taste of what you have to offer and a reason to continue to follow and learn from you. Because a lead magnet is your chance to make a first impression, it should address your target market's biggest struggle and solve at least one problem for them.

Ask yourself if you would pay for the content in your freebie. If the answer is yes, you're good to go.

If you haven't started **guest posting**, what are you waiting for? Guest posting has been one of the best ways to grow not only my list, but my credibility.

Guest posting is perfect if you have a small following and not many people visit your site daily.

Contributing to someone else's blog gives you the opportunity to leverage their super-engaged audience. You will be exposed to hundreds, if not thousands, of people who would never know about you otherwise.

You can also **run a free limited-time challenge** using the 2 social media platforms you chose earlier in this chapter.

Every time I run a free challenge, I grow my list by HUNDREDS of people. Challenges can last 5-10 days and are more results-oriented than the previous list-building techniques. You want your newest followers to experience a small win by completing the challenge. This gets them excited about future opportunities. At the same time, the challenge gives potential clients a taste of what it's like to work with you and learn from you.

What do people care about the most in your industry? Weight loss? Confidence? Successful launches? Turn that into a challenge, and watch your list double in size, then double again!

And finally, because the content creation wheels have started to turn in your head by now, I want you to capitalize on all of the posts you'll be writing and sharing.

Feature some sort of **call-to-action button** at the bottom or on the side of every blog post you publish. For social media, include a link whenever you post.

Having a call-to-action that sends viewers to your subscription form is a great way to build your list effortlessly with people who are *already* interested in what you have to say. You don't want to miss the opportunity to get current readers onto your list.

SIMPLE SOCIAL INFLUENCE

I know this gives you a LOT to think about!

Like I wrote earlier, the point is not to try everything I say once, then give up because you worked 'til 4 in the morning on planning your authority positioning content.

The point is, if you want to make an impact on your tribe and influence them for good, you have to be consistent.

And you have to be confident. If you're not super freaking confident about what you're doing, change it.

So to close out this chapter—and to heave this fourth of eight doors wide open for you, for good—I want you to write down a declaration.

This is your power statement that will motivate you to power through any writer's block that strikes and any symptoms of imposter syndrome that creep in. Write:

"I am _____ and I am THE go to expert for _____."

Fill in those blanks, and repeat that sentence to yourself verbally into the mirror when you wake up every day.

Start your mornings by recognizing the influencer who your 1,000 True Fans will be giving all the credit for their success to:

You.

I'll see you at the fifth door.

CHAPTER 5

Killer Content Creation

When it comes to content, you have one chance to make a lasting impression. Give it all you've got!

Halfway.

You're halfway now.

Yes, you've walked with me through four of our eight doors.

But that does NOT mean you are only *halfway to freedom.*

Each door—from "Your New Operating System" to "Simple Social Influence"—is a means to freedom in and of itself.

But just as an online business doesn't run on only a single successful launch and that's it, so there is MORE freedom available to you.

And not just freedom FROM the darkness of doubt, worry and fear, but freedom TO do things like influence others, enjoy rockstar confidence and transform new subscribers into repeat buyers.

KILLER CONTENT CREATION

Here in Chapter 5, you're going to find freedom to create KILLER content that entertains, educates and excites your Tribe. Killer content positions you as the only and obvious choice for potential buyers.

Yes, we touched on this last chapter, but there is a grand strategy to motivate website visitors and social followers to become engaged subscribers and who, in turn, become clients or customers.

And that grand strategy is the topic of this chapter. So let's get right to the good stuff!

The fact is, content marketing has been the #1 driver of new business for me. According to Demand Gen, businesses that invest time and effort into content marketing—like creating lead magnets and designing follow-up funnels that send subscribers even more solid content—enjoy 6 TIMES more conversions than businesses that don't.

That's a wake-up call to entrepreneurs who think they can skate by with a few social media posts a month, a lead magnet they threw together in an afternoon and an email blast here and another there.

WRONG!

Content marketing that WORKS is all about creating relevant, viable and value-driven content that becomes the inspiration for viral shares and unsolicited referrals.

So, enough of the hustle. Let's create such good shit that people cannot help but come to you FIRST.

We want to affect lives. We want to show that we have original approaches and ideas that will compel potential clients and turn them into not only buyers but raving fans.

At the end of Chapter 4, I described the *where* of getting readers to become subscribers by using email list opt-in forms, so now it's time for the *how*. As in...

How you are going to get people to fall head-over-fucking-heels in love with you so that subscribing to your list is a decision they don't even have to make.

I hinted at the answer last chapter—stellar lead magnets.

But what exactly are these things? 5-page PDF documents with random tips off Google? Hell no!

Not all opt-in freebies are created equal. If there is one part of your business that I would consider responsible for the financial momentum of big leaps, it is the intensity and execution with which you create and disseminate opt-ins.

Lead magnets are your chance to make a lasting first impression on your potential clients. This ability to truly share your genius with the proper intention will pave a road of very happy and willing-to-pay followers.

Rather than kicking off the lead magnet creation process with a peek at what the big names in your industry are doing, start with what matters most to your ideal buyers FIRST.

What are their immediate needs? What challenge or frustration—if solved—would pave the way for them to become your customers?

KILLER CONTENT CREATION

In what ways can you make your best ideas easily digestible in just a few minutes of reading, watching or listening? What "wins" could you help them achieve that would produce noticeable results instantly?

What free material from your entry-level product or main offering could you repurpose as a lead magnet worth subscribing to your list to get ahold of?

Once answers materialize for those questions, consider YOUR behavior when it comes to lead magnets. What have been YOUR favorites? What did you get out of them? What changed for you?

And of course, what were your LEAST favorite lead magnets? What did you hate? In what ways were they confusing or time-wasting?

Answers to questions like these will hone your focus on the content that needs to appear in your lead magnets.

Next, you need to give thought to the medium of choice. Take your pick from this short list, or come up with your own:

- Mini Course
- Video Series
- eBook
- Cheat Sheet
- Checklist
- Planner
- Done-For-You Template
- Resource List
- Case Study
- Assessment

Just as man shall not live by bread alone, so a one-woman business shall not live by freebies alone.

Consider your stellar lead magnets the tip of your iceberg of profit—there HAS to be a lot more beneath the surface, or that *iceberg* is just an *icicle*.

Lead magnets are just a sample of what is to come, and that is exactly the point of what I want to show you next—there MUST be more to come!

What I'm getting at is called "The Customer's Journey", and it's the strategy that takes subscribers from being interested in your free lead magnet, to being OBSESSED about your products and services.

How do we do it? By retooling the idea of sales funnels.

I know, I know... Sales funnels are the soulless way to get money in the bank. Maybe you've thought that, at least.

In reality, a sales funnel driven by The Customer's Journey strategy allows you to meet your audience where they are every stage of the game, give them exactly what they need and attract more sales than you ever would have otherwise.

Ultimately, you never want your people to feel like just another number or just another email to spam. My re-imagining of the sales funnel allows you to create relationships with prospects that convey your commitment to them while also being authentic to yourself and your beliefs.

Just as importantly, it's sustainable and keeps the money flowing.

KILLER CONTENT CREATION

Every Customer Journey-based sales funnel starts with a stellar lead magnet and continues with a welcome email. That's **day one**.

In your welcome email, you introduce yourself and give subscribers the link to the free lead magnet you promised. Mention your entry-level product in the P.S. of this email so that "I need a solution RIGHT NOW" type subscribers can become new customers immediately.

On **day two**, deliver more high-value content in your email. I recommend repurposing and expanding on one of your Simple Social Influence posts you worked on in the previous chapter and making that the topic of your email.

As you close out this email, briefly offer a preview of your main product or primary service—you'll be going into more depth tomorrow.

Then in your **third email**, REALLY lean in for the ask. But use testimonial-driven social proof to showcase WHY others in the past chose to work with you or buy your programs.

At this point, yes you're selling, but you're offering high-value content to people within the funnel.

In the **fourth email**, it's time to get personal. Help them identify with YOU by identifying with THEM. Speak heart to heart about why you do not want them to miss out on the results they can experience through your product or service.

On **day five**, ask your subscribers if they're in or out. If they believe enough is enough, and they can't go on without fulfilling their goal or solving their problem one more day, there's no reason to NOT whip out that credit card.

From this point on in the funnel, you separate the buyers from the non-buyers. Anyone who purchases goes right into your next email sequence to get acquainted with you and your program, while subscribers who don't buy move to a nurture sequence in which they receive your regular email updates and any new lead magnets you create.

It's literally that simple. No sleaze, no bullshit, no guilt.

By being straightforward with your subscribers about what you're selling and why—and by combining that with content that really is worth paying for in and of itself—you're officially a creator of KILL-ER content.

Now, about that course your subscribers just bought in your sales funnel...

What is it? How do you create it? And how do you make sure people actually go through it and get results without feeling overwhelmed?

Like my Customer Journey-driven sales funnel, my course development process is equally simple.

Instead of 5 days, it's 3 stages.

The **first stage** of course development is choosing your big idea. If you're in digital marketing, then will your program focus on high-converting authority blogging, eye-catching graphic design for social media or email copy that sells sleaze-free?

Pick one and go with it.

For the **second stage**, identify which problems you're going to solve. If you, a digital marketing consultant, decide that your next program is going to cover high-converting authority blogging, then what are the biggest challenges that your clients have with writing blog posts that attract readers?

Each problem you want to solve should have its own module or lesson associated with it where you teach HOW to solve that individual problem once and for all.

And THAT gets into the **third stage**—actually creating the course content for each lesson or module.

Following the digital marketing example, let's say that one of the problems you want to solve is blogger's block, AKA writer's block for B2B bloggers.

You have a main idea—how to overcome blogger's block and create share-worthy content for your business blog.

From there, you need to have at least 3 sub-ideas that—when implemented—lead directly to the outcome of overcoming blogger's block, which in turn leads directly to the benefits of producing more content that potential clients can enjoy than they EVER have before.

Repeat this third step for as many modules or lessons your course needs, and you're all set to launch a course people will be MORE than happy to pay for!

Depending on your industry, you may want to launch 1 new program a quarter, or you may need to open up your 1:1 Coaching spots once every year.

YOUR FIRST SIX FIGURES

The point of developing a content marketing strategy that combines stellar lead magnets with The Customer's Journey strategy and products people buy is not to promote, promote, promote and sell, sell, sell.

You're in business to create results. To make change. To LEAD.

Every time you publish a new lead magnet, write a new sales funnel email or launch a new offering, you are choosing to lead—whether you have 1,000 subscribers or 1 million.

Being a leader means being the one whose message sticks in people's minds and makes them think, "Hey, me too! I believe in that, too! I stand for that, too! I want to be a part of that, too!"

Then through both free and paid content, you allow your Tribe to become a part of your movement.

Remember, it's YOUR movement here. It's YOUR customers' journey, no one else's. Don't feel like you have to do what everyone else is doing or copy every single aspect of what the gurus of your niche are doing content marketing-wise.

Really, success in content creation and in your business overall comes down to what you want to get out of them.

Maybe you don't want to make $100,000 every few weeks and go on retreats in Bali like I do. Good for you! OWN that. Maybe you just want to make enough money to stay home with your kids and take them on vacation a couple times a year, or to replace your 9-5 income so you can finally quit.

KILLER CONTENT CREATION

Whatever you want, the best thing you can do is hop off the bandwagons of fairy dust and unicorns and be REAL. That's what I do—with the content I create, with the messages I send out to the world, with the goals I set for myself.

And guess what, it's worked! People appreciate me for being real, for being honest and for giving without expecting anything in return.

That level of authenticity will keep readers soaking every word you write into their consciousness more than any cleverly titled shitpost of an ebook EVER will.

You want rapport with your readers. True connection with your audience. Real relationships with your Tribe.

When it comes to everything you do with content to grow your business, I cannot stress it enough—it's never about YOU, it's about THEM.

To create raving fans like I have, show up and over-deliver.

Again.

And again.

And again.

People need to know who you are, how you can help them and what makes you different. But you must give away your best content. If you give away junk in your lead magnets and the welcome emails that follow, no one will ever pay you for your products or services.

And that's a fact.

When you give away good stuff, you get known as a credible source, you become liked and you are deemed trustworthy

Even if doubters and naysayers unsubscribe by the dozens during your first (or next) launch, I want you to have courage.

You see, we're trained from childhood to seek approval. Anything outside of the norm is taboo. Toss that limited thinking to the side and start creating the content you want, on your terms.

And don't just write about your collection of success stories, FLAUNT them! Show them off! Get people to see them!

I don't care where you're at in your business right now, whether you have created 2 lead magnets or 200.

Authentic content marketing that shows off everything AMAZING you are to the world requires perseverance.

I can give you all the best ideas I've got, but they don't mean anything unless you keep going, keep creating, keep sharing.

Success with content really is a numbers game. The more people you connect with, the more potential clients you have. And even if you're not a perfect fit for certain people, you still want to show up and add value because you never know who they know. They could recommend you to friends, call you out when someone is looking for someone in your specific field or they could even potentially be someone you collaborate with in the future. Don't underestimate the power of relationships.

To wrap up this chapter in the simplest way possible, I'll put it to you like this—you know that your killer content truly is killer when more and more people come to know, like and trust you every single day.

To get people to KNOW you, show the fuck up. Apply everything you learned in Chapter 4 about consistent social media posting. Create lead magnets people care about, and get them into your email sequences.

To get people to LIKE you, just be you. Likability isn't about popularity or following the crowd. You create likability through your demeanor, your value, your gifts and your genuine interest in others. Be vulnerable, share your stories, share your struggles and share your successes.

To get people to TRUST you, do what you say you're going to do. Because people are watching. If you say you're going to send a newsletter out every week, then send one out every week. If you want people to join your online community or follow you on social media, post regularly, engage with your audience and over-deliver in the areas where your competition under-delivers.

Online success is all about building relationships and nurturing them.

I want you to have as many of them as possible.

Because the truth is, people don't buy your products or services—they buy YOU.

If there's anything I want to help you do as a result of this chapter—and this book, really—it's this:

I want you to sell the SHIT out of you.

Deal?

CHAPTER 6
Social Amplification

Do your own thing. Be different. Be great. Find your secret sauce. And don't forget to flip on your OPEN sign so people know they can come in and BUY...from YOU.

"But Jenn! I'm writing emails... I'm publishing posts on social media... I'm creating lead magnets... So why do I STILL only have fifty subscribers?!"

This is a complaint that I'm going to nip in the bud—or even BEFORE it buds.

I'm going to get into this point later, but it is worth mentioning now:

You don't graduate with your degree after a single class.

And you won't have a 6-figure or 7-figure business after reading a few chapters of this book.

YES everything you've learned so far is important.

YES writing emails is critical to product launch success.

YES consistently putting content out there on social media is a requirement for reaching new people.

YOUR FIRST SIX FIGURES

YES stellar lead magnets are the single best way to turn browsers into subscribers, and eventually those subscribers into buyers.

But if you only have 10 people a day coming into your funnel, guess what?

You'll be lucky if you get a single sale.

Sister, you need some amplification. The fastest way to reach a thousand sales is to have thousands of people coming your way!

And posting a meme on Instagram once a day with your smiling face will not do the trick.

That's why the sixth doorway to freedom is the most important one yet.

Like lined-up dominoes falling onto each other, you do NOT want the chain to be broken. If one domino in the line doesn't fall onto the next, that piece has failed every single one that came before it in the line.

And if there's one thing I will NOT let happen to your business, it is this kind of failure—knowing and doing all the right things EXCEPT for that one thing which would multiply all of your previous efforts to produce the results you've worked so hard to achieve.

I'm not the kind of coach to leave that piece out, and I'm not that kind of author either.

That's why you're getting an ENTIRE chapter dedicated to amplifying your reach, raising your visibility and multiplying your influence.

SOCIAL AMPLIFICATION

The world is not going to buy from you if the world doesn't know your name. So I'm going to show you how to reach as many people as possible with your message and catapult yourself into the league of your industry's giants.

If you're time-starved, one of the fastest ways to do that is to launch a social challenge.

You've seen me mention these briefly before—the "what"—so now this chapter is the ideal place to dig into the steps of making challenges happen—the "how".

If you're a health coach, a social challenge like "Lose 5 pounds in 5 days" is a great start, but your audience deserves more creativity, something with depth that makes them think, "Wow, I totally want those results! Count me in!"

As you plan your first (or next) social challenge, ask yourself a few questions:

- What does my audience need to know or do BEFORE they buy my main offer?
- Which social media channels are likely to get the most organic shares, re-posts, re-pins or retweets?
- What competitive elements can I bring into the challenge? What prizes can contestants win?
- What lead magnet(s) can I give away at the start of the challenge to courage opt-in's?
- How long will the social challenge last and when will I start promoting it?

YOUR FIRST SIX FIGURES

If you don't do a single other thing to plan your social challenge, I want you to answer these questions—they're non-negotiable for running a challenge that produces MASSIVE increases for your subscriber, fan and follower count.

How do I know this?

Because I've done it myself MANY times.

Before social challenges were even a thing, I was running them—starting back in March 2014.

Since then, I've hosted over two dozen challenges and added over 16,000 people to my audience. Not bad for something that cost me nothing but a few hours of time!

As quick pointers, I recommend that you run yours for only 5-7 days. That is the average participant's attention span for something like this.

And the first time you do a challenge, do NOT send people directly into an upsell as soon as the challenge is complete. That's just tacky.

You want to build that goodwill and increase your likeability to new people, so share with them your best free content—blog articles, social media posts, lead magnets, etc.—for the first few weeks after your challenge is wrapped.

If you're on a second or third challenge, then sending participants directly into a product launch of service enrollment funnel is a wise move.

You *can* supplement the organic growth of your launch with ads that send people to the Facebook group you create for hosting your challenge, but I prefer to promote my upcoming challenges through guest posts and guest podcast interviews. (I'll explain these tactics in a few pages.)

At this point, I know some readers are thinking, "No way challenges can be THAT easy!"

And you're right—at least, not if you don't know what pitfalls to watch out for.

Having seen SO many social challenges fall off the cliff into oblivion and irrelevance within the first couple of days, I know what to watch out for—and what to want you about.

First of all, it's important to make sure your participants make it all the way through the challenge itself, ESPECIALLY if you plan to promote something at the end.

If they can't make it through your challenge, chances are high that they won't purchase or bite on what you offer.

That's why I ALWAYS create a private Facebook group for my social challenges and encourage everyone to post their progress DAILY. When you the host do publish a post in the group, mix it up—use text-based posts, images and even videos to keep everyone engaged for that critical 5-7 day period.

Then there is the ultimate failure of social challenges—not planning them at all! If you aren't regularly surveying the audience you do have or aren't keeping tabs on trends in your market, then you'll create a challenge you "think" people will enjoy, but no one ACTUALLY wants.

The result? Very few people will sign up, and you will see very little engagement from those who do.

For example, if you're a personal trainer, do NOT run a challenge like "30 days to burning 100 extra calories per workout."

It's too long, and your promised results are paltry compared to what someone in your audience WOULD believe is worth 30 days of continual effort to attain.

So once you DO have a challenge that will motivate the masses to jump on it, promote the hell out of it for 7-14 days prior to the challenge start date—especially if you have a social following of fewer than 500 people.

And whatever you do, DO NOT turn your social challenge into your personal headache. Overcomplicating things has got to be the WORST mistake I see. Too much text in your updates, too many tasks to accomplish in a day, too much content in your initial challenge directions...don't do it.

Otherwise, your ideal peeps will become angry patrons who regret having committed to ANYTHING with your name on it.

SO when you think about creating a challenge, think simple. What can you ask participants to do that is downright easy to implement and achieve results—as long as they have directions from an engaged challenge host?

Do that. Keep it simple, sister. Make each day one actionable step—two if they complement each other—and leave it at that.

SOCIAL AMPLIFICATION

I do have a word of caution on this:

The point of social challenges is NOT to give away the farm.

The point is to have newcomers to your brand feel motivated to take small actions that lead to much bigger results—results worth sticking around to see more of what you've got to offer.

You've got to remember, we live in a society where instant gratification is the norm. So cut out all the fluff and make your daily challenge prompts clear and concise, leading DIRECTLY to a tangible result that they can brag about to others.

Pounds lost. Inches decreased. Hours saved. Clients gained. Leads generated. Profits increased. Goals accomplished. Tasks delegated.

The entire point of the challenge is to have people actually finish it and get a specific result.

Now, once you've mastered the art and science of running social challenges with total-strangers-turned-raving-fans, consider yourself ready to move to the next level of social amplification:

Building credibility with *other* people's audiences.

In short, it's time to launch joint venture partnerships.

I'm talking about MUCH more than tossing affiliate links around like a sleazy internet promoter circa 2003—I mean being a true PARTNER to people who already have sizeable audiences that would have otherwise taken you YEARS to build working by yourself.

Joint venture partnerships are perfect if you already have a product created, even if it is $50 or less.

Typically, joint venture partners expect AT LEAST 40% of the profit from each sale to their audience.

However, to pique the curiosity of anyone with any influence in your industry, your pitch HAS to be more creative than, "Hey you! Wanna take half the revenue from selling my shit for me?"

When you reach out to potential partners via social media or email, weave your answers to the following questions into your value-driven pitch:

- How will their audience benefit from your product?
- What will their audience get from you that they haven't anywhere else?
- Are there any "gaps" in the knowledge strategies that your potential JV partner hasn't yet filled for their audience?
- Why is your product ideal for that particular JV partner to promote?

Even if you don't yet have a product to sell to another's audience, you can promote a joint webinar or swap lead magnets. That will just as easily move more people to your list than you ever have before.

Another format for JV partnerships is the online summit.

With a summit, you schedule a series of webinars that all reflect a similar theme relevant to both your audience AND your potential summit co-hosts.

SOCIAL AMPLIFICATION

You can interview each partner for the summit or ask them to create a solo webinar that covers some of their best material.

Then, everyone who participates in the summit shares the summit opt-in link with their audiences, and your subscriber count EXPLODES overnight.

Plus, every co-host benefits by having their brands cross-promoted to everyone else's audiences that participates.

Win-win-win!

Continuing with this theme of collaborative content creation, I want to shift gears slightly and cruise through another way to amplify your social reach, influence and following:

Guest posts and guest podcast interviews.

This approach is the #1 way for total newbies to build brand authority and credibility.

Anywhere from 2 to 10 times per month, you want your name and your ideas to appear on an industry influencer's website, blog, show or podcast.

Most websites worth a damn have guest post submission forms, so that takes care of that concern. The easiest way I've found to get accepted is two-fold—follow EVERY step of their submission guidelines and pitch an idea that has NOT appeared on their website before (at least not anytime recently).

You want to introduce fresh, new, relevant ideas to your audience—and so does the website's content gatekeeper.

YOUR FIRST SIX FIGURES

When you DO get accepted, congratulations! This is where the real fun begins...

If you aren't the greatest writer on the planet, record yourself talking through an outline of the post and get it transcribed by Rev.com for $1 per minute. Then hire an editor on Fiverr.com and you're all set!

In your guest author bio, include a hyperlink to your lead magnet opt-in page.

It really is that easy to turn readers into subscribers by the dozens and hundreds.

For guest podcasting interviews, start small. To sound more natural, start with podcasts of friends and peers you already know.

Once you've gotten a few interviews under your belt, it will be MUCH easier to calm your nerves when you're chatting with a top-tier influencer in your niche whose audience numbers in the HUNDREDS of thousands—or more.

For every guest post you write and every guest podcast interview you record, include that site's or show's logo on your website to establish credibility and trustworthiness to incoming traffic.

If you're reading this thinking, "Great! So what should I pitch to these people?" start your authentic self-promotion journey by brainstorming a good 10-20 topics.

What unique stories, proven strategies or contrarian viewpoints will make you THE must-feature guest?

Write those down and turn them into a 2-3 sentence pitch you can submit over and over and over to the top blogs, websites, shows and podcasts in your niche.

Leverage every successful post and interview to score another one—keep that social amplification going and soon you'll find your audience size doubling, tripling and quadrupling every month, every week, even every DAY. (Yes, I had this happen several times in my early days of business after an interview went live on the web.)

Sure, you can create an ENORMOUS reach by implementing these strategies for social challenges, joint venture partnerships, guest blogs and guest podcast interviews.

But I want you to think bigger, a LOT bigger. The more wantrepreneurs who dip their toes into the murky waters of online business, the more of them will be trying the easier stuff—like publishing on social media, launching entry level products and pitching blogs with a few hundred subscribers.

I want MORE for you than that. And by walking through this sixth door of freedom with me, I know that you do, too.

So start your own podcast. iTunes' free tutorial makes it easier than ever before. Inexpensive services like Libsyn allow you to host and publish new episodes for only a few bucks per month.

If you live or work in or near a city, why not host live events, workshops and seminars? You can either charge a small fee for these events or host them for free, then sell your services at the end just like would during a webinar.

YOUR FIRST SIX FIGURES

Since you can easily get 2-5 new clients per event—even with only a dozen attendees—this is an ideal social amplification tactic for services-based entrepreneurs.

Like being in front of people? Continue this theme of offline promotion by booking speaking gigs. Polished, professional, value-driven speaking is a VERY lucrative arm of the coaching industry.

You can get paid anywhere from $500 to $5,000 for a single speaking engagement or keynote address! Imagine just doing ONE of these per month. It's totally possible—in fact, one of my dear friends has over 40 speaking engagements booked this year.

Or you can follow another set of my footsteps by writing, publishing and promoting books and ebooks—MULTIPLE books and ebooks, that is. If you prefer to write instead of speak or teach in front of a live audience, then write your heart out, sister!

With the invention of self-publishing and Amazon's intuitive CreateSpace platform, there is no excuse for NOT adding books and ebooks to your library of social amplification strategies. (Pun intended.)

You can even pop a short 50-page ebook into Amazon's Short Reads programs to start making money off of your words faster than has EVER been possible before in human history. One of my mentors writes at least one book PER MONTH.

Plus, you don't even have to go solo—work with a ghostwriter; sketch out a rough outline and hire an editor; or record your ideas, get them transcribed and touch up the content to make it final draft-ready.

SOCIAL AMPLIFICATION

Although not as in-depth as writing and publishing books, corporate coaching is another great reach-the-masses tactic—specifically if you work in the field of mindset, leadership and organization.

You can be paid VERY handsomely to coach corporate clients and small businesses' staff. These gigs are usually contracted outside of the organization itself, so you can expect to earn a hefty up-front fee to work with executives, management, employees or interns.

So now, there's no excuse!

In just a few short pages, I've given you EVERY tool imaginable to turn a tiny audience into an explosive tribe of crazy word-of-mouth marketers, to transform a small list of freebie-hunting subscribers into a mob of credit card-swiping customers.

The only question left is, which tactic to amplify your reach will you put to use first?

CHAPTER 7

Sleaze-Free Selling

God did not put you on this Earth to be broke and struggling. He put you here to shine, to share your gifts, to impact others and to speak your truth.

Sales:

If you don't have them, you don't have a business. Period.

That being said, the last thing I want you to become after reading this book is the internet's equivalent of a door-to-door vacuum cleaner salesman, where anything you come across that breathes you consider a qualified lead whether or not you (or they) even know if they're in your target market. Lame.

"Sleaze-Free Selling"—our seventh door of freedom—is THE difference between struggling with the bare minimum of making it by and owning your niche while turning a fucking AMAZING profit every single month.

So we'd better do it right.

SLEAZE-FREE SELLING

Look, selling doesn't have to be sleazy—*looking at you, 1950's vacuum salesman*.

In fact, selling is NEVER sleazy when you believe 100% in yourself, your mission, your brand and your offering.

With your new Operating System (mindset), you're in a different zone of belief now. You can look at everything you bring to the table, from natural talent and years of experience to the accomplishments you've achieved for yourself and your clients and customers.

Sister, you've got MAD value to offer to this world, and there's no reason for you to hide it.

So sell, baby, sell!

Since launching my first beta product for less than the cost of a fast-casual meal, I've scaled up to the highest of high end 1:1 Coaching business models.

During that adventure, I've learned one truth that gets ignored by 99% of the business owners who started where I did...but never made it beyond that.

Selling is downright EASY when you can get your prospect to believe in your product as much as you do.

Sure, that sounds simple—but actually doing that is far from elementary.

Creating sales is more than just blasting off email after email, assuming people on your list will buy your new product simply because you've got 2-3 testimonials for it.

119

I want you to be magnetic in your sales, maximizing your profits when launching your programs and services.

And that means taking what you've learned so far in this book about creating products you KNOW your audience will love, promoting them with the right kinds of emotionally engaging content and taking a position of credible authority to get noticed on the right social channels.

But to turn a product launch funnel into a 24/7/365 sales-generating machine—that requires a slightly more sophisticated structure.

And THAT is the topic of Chapter 7. Because when it comes to selling, selling more and selling often, there is a specific method to approaching your audience and asking for the sale that turns relationships into revenue.

Like I've hinted at so far at the beginning of this chapter, the secret has to do with understanding why your prospects NEED your product and how to show the value in your offer.

Having learned from the best in the business, I am going to offer you a behind-the-scenes look at launching from a leadership perspective that gets money into your bank account without feeling like a spammer—because you're not.

Now, before you launch your first (or next) product or service, you've got some planning to do. Since every sleaze-free sale starts with the value that YOU have to offer the world, the right plan is the natural place to start.

SLEAZE-FREE SELLING

The most effective pre-launch plans are those that cover a few critical questions which, if not answered, will wreak havoc as your launch progresses. You don't want that.

So start with the size of your launch.

At what scale do you want to launch? Are we talking an all-out blitz of every promotional channel you have available—and the corresponding time and money you'll have to invest—or do you want to keep things under-the-radar and launch only to a small list of subscribers, your current social media following and past clients and customers who may be interested in an upsell?

How long do you want your launch to last? The #1 sleaziest sales tactic on the planet is to engage in a perpetually infinite barrage of "Buy Now! Buy Now! Buy Now!" messages.

Do. Not. Do. That.

Instead, select a Cart Open date and a Cart Closed date. Structure your stellar lead magnet deployment and guest posting around those dates.

Or, for low to medium priced products, you can go with the Evergreen model. With this product launch format, you are using a combination of Facebook ads, free traffic and guest posts and interviews to send new subscribers into your product launch.

But only ONCE.

Just once.

Don't be the broken record of sales, emailing the same tired pitch to the same people over and over again. Once a new subscriber enters your Evergreen launch funnel, they receive your product emails.

If they buy, great! If not, perhaps another product. Respect their space, whatever decision they make.

The fact is, there ARE going to be people—the majority of people, in fact—who are just not yet ready for your product or service.

Maybe it's not the right time, it's not in their budget or they're still in the middle of realizing that they need your brilliance in their lives or businesses in the first place.

That said, I want you to set your launch goals during this pre-launch process—Good, Better and Best.

For example, if you're launching your third product to an engaged list of 10,000 people, you can set your Good goal at 0.5%. This means you'll still feel good about your launch even if only 50 people become customers.

For premium products, 50 new sales can easily surpass the average 9-to-5 person's entire ANNUAL income.

For a Better goal, let's say your number is 1.5%—or 150 total new customers.

And for your Best goal, feel free to get a little crazy, WAY crazy even. Following my example, you'd aim for 5% of your entire list to buy on this launch. That's 500 total sales!

If your product is $2,000 or above, guess what? You officially have a 7-figure business!

That's the beauty—and the profit—of sales done right.

Plan for success, and you will not easily be swayed off-course.

I know these pre-launch questions give you a LOT to think about. The good news is, there's no right or wrong answer to any of them—well, there IS a wrong answer, and that wrong answer is not having any!

So even if you have to put this book down and journal your ideas (Remember Chapter 1?) then do exactly that. Your future bank account will be forever grateful.

My method to creating a magnetic offer doesn't end there. Like you did in Chapter 1, get inside the head of your ideal prospect to make an irresistible offer they can't say no to.

Whether you're selling a $50 audiobook, a $50,000 Done-For-You service or a $500 video course, realize one thing about the people who will ultimately buy from you:

Right now, they're *HERE*. But they want to be *THERE*.

As you write the sales page copy and product launch emails, drive this point home:

Your offering will transport customers from where they ARE—and everything they struggle with related to your niche—to where they desperately

WANT to be—where every solution they dreamed of is delivered to them on a silver platter.

Tell that tale. Weave that story. Create that narrative.

I don't care how famous you are, nobody is going to buy an ecourse from you (or me) because they like the modules' fancy titles, appreciate the HD video quality or enjoy printing off PDF worksheets.

HOWEVER...

The right people in your target market WILL happily part with every last expendable cent they have if your product can move them from the oh-so-painful HERE...to the oh-so-pleasurable THERE.

I know this may sound theoretical, so let me give you a tip on how to demonstrate HOW your product or service will do this.

Take out a piece of paper or open a blank document.

Create two columns. Label the left column "Features" and label the right column "Benefits".

Next, jot down every feature your product or service has. Then in the corresponding column, write what that feature's corresponding "transporting" benefit is.

Here's what I mean by the word "transporting".

If I'm launching a 1:1 Coaching program, one of the features of my services is accountability. But what exactly is the "transporting" benefit of accountability?

When I write the sales page copy, I would say something like:

"I will hold you accountable to completing every growth-oriented task you set your mind to. This guarantees you consistently implement everything you learn from our work together and NEVER fall back into the habits that put you where you are now."

See the difference?

A generic feature becomes a gotta-have-it benefit that hundreds of people have paid me handsomely for (and will do the same for you).

So when you describe what your product or services include, make it your #1 copywriting goal to describe how each feature will move your prospects from HERE to THERE with speed and ease.

Once you've nailed the content that promotes your product, you are all set for a lucrative launch.

In Chapter 3, I covered the different types of offerings you can create for your target market when you DO launch. And in Chapters 4 and 5, you learned how to crank out KILLER content that turns browsers into buyers.

So to keep things moving, I won't rehash what you've already seen. Instead, I want to share with you the wisdom that I did NOT have the first few times I launched, costing me tens of thousands of dollars each and every time. (Ouch.)

One of these simple tips I had no clue I needed to embrace?

Don't rush it.

YOUR FIRST SIX FIGURES

Whether you're launching a product to an audience of 100 or 100,000 for the first of fifteenth time, be methodical. Give yourself enough time for pre-launch planning and content marketing.

Nowadays, when I launch a new program—or advise others to—I insist on a MINIMUM of 6-8 weeks of prep work.

One of the most important parts of this prep work is deciding how to reward the early birds—the people who sign up right away, who ask you for the link to the sales page before you've finished it, who email you with reasons why YOU need to let THEM buy from you.

Yes, that actually happens!

These peeps are part of your 1,000 True Fans that I wrote about in Chapter 1! They are decisive. They know they want it. If it's got your name on it, their credit card belongs to you—and they're okay with admitting it.

Devote time during your 6-8 weeks of pre-launch planning to create exclusive bonuses ONLY available to these True Fans.

If you're launching an ecourse, offer early bird customers a complimentary 30-minute coaching call with you.

If you're opening up a few spots for Done-For-You services, toss in an additional service that you normally charge for, at no extra cost.

Whether your early bird special runs for 2 weeks prior to launch or for 2 hours before the cart officially opens, make sure your rewards are worth scrambling for!

That also means urgency needs to play a factor—both with the early bird special AND the launch length itself.

Giving subscribers a month and a half to access your bonus and then leaving the cart open for 3 whole weeks—both of these are launch goal-destroyers in the making.

Long launches give people too much time to think, to talk themselves out of it or to just forget about it altogether! Plus, keeping the cart open too long makes you more stressed out about the launch. *Lose-lose.*

As you do your due diligence to avoid such a disaster and exceed the launch goals you set, pull out all the stops.

Don't tip-toe through this seventh doorway to freedom like someone's going to catch you.

FLY through!

Selling without excuses—and launching without doubts—isn't just about telling people that your new product is live once or twice and hoping people jump all over it.

Like I mentioned earlier, get people EXCITED. This can mean doing a webinar (or a series of them), publishing a daily video (and getting people to comment and share) or running a social media challenge (or posting worth-paying-for content from your program in your free Facebook group).

Sleaze-free selling requires you to show how passionate and pure your motivations are. If you don't LOOK excited, people will smell the stench of inauthenticity a thousand miles away.

On the other hand, the more you are excited about your product or service, the more your potential purchasers will be, too.

Notice that you just read, "...or service" in the sentence above.

That's another thing I learned from miscues, missteps and mistakes early on in my career—the fact that selling a service is not *quite* the same as selling a product.

I'd be doing you no favors by leaving out the same piece that is missing from just about every internet marketing-related book, program, course and training available today:

How exactly do you turn inbox-to-inbox subscribers into face-to-face clients?

Of course, face-to-face can mean working with individual clients—or groups of them—via video chat, phone or a membership site (or a combination of all 3).

What differentiates selling a service from selling a product is how personal your offering really is. (Duh.)

Harkening back to Chapter 4 for a second...

People don't just buy your services, they buy YOU.

The 3 tactics to turn subscribers into clients that get overlooked time and time again are leveraging testimonials, following up with "not yet" prospects and completely fucking up your pricing.

As for testimonials, yes, we all know how critical social proof is to the success of any launch.

But for launching services *specifically*, testimonials, case studies and success stories of lives or businesses transformed through 1:1 work with you are the lifeblood of sleaze-free selling.

If you cannot look (or talk) to a prospect and say, "The results you will pay me a heck of a lot of money to achieve, I've already helped Client ABC and Client XYZ accomplish. You can trust me," it will be excruciatingly hard to persuade.

It may not feel like discovery calls are THAT black and white—and yet they are.

Nobody will pay you $1,000 to make back $999 worth of value.

So unless your prospect is 100% convinced that they are in good hands with you, your prospect is 100% convinced that you are bullshitting them.

Even when you do share stories of clients who you brought from THERE to HERE through 1:1 services, not everyone you reach in your launch is going to be ready to hire you right away.

In the same way that you send non-buying subscribers into a nurturing sequence (Chapter 4), place non-hiring prospects into a similar one.

Keep your services—and the ROI they produce—top of mind over the coming weeks and months, and when prospects ARE ready, you'll be the first and only business owner they think of.

Now, a word on pricing your services...

More specifically, 2 words—those 2 words being, "fuck" followed by "it".

Seriously, the advice you have probably gotten about charging by the hour, calculating a salary-like wage and obeying the utterly nonspecific "what the market will pay" rule are total shit.

How do I know this?

Because I followed that advice—ALL of it.

Guess what I learned?

Whenever I attempted to "own my worth" and implement the so-called experts' pricing strategies, I heard one of two excuses from prospects over and over.

Can you guess what they were?

I'll give you a hint—one of them had to do with charging too much that they couldn't afford me, while the other had to do with charging too little that they couldn't respect me.

See the problem?

My services pricing frustrations—and yours too, I'm sure—all stem from following other people's advice.

If there is a single rule you DO want to follow when it comes to pricing, it's this—charge whatever the hell you want.

Seriously.

Pick a number.

Then let your prospects decide if it's fair for the value you offer in exchange.

If EVERYONE jumps on it without question or qualms, you know it's too low.

And if NO ONE hires you because you're charging more than your mentors, you know it's too high.

Pricing isn't complicated, sister—we only make it that way by implementing ideas fit for the waste basket.

It's YOUR job to know your value and stand by it. Don't be wishy-washy about your pricing and what you offer when faced with someone else's shitty money story.

If you want to charge $5,000 for a service, then charge $5,000!

If you only want to charge $2,000, then do that. Do what feels good to you...

...AND what feels good to your audience.

If you are marketing to brand new coaches or single moms and your prices are $5,000+ for a single service, chances are they aren't going to be able to afford it.

That's why, to attract the caliber of client you want, I recommend creating a "Top 10 Reasons You Should Never Work With Me" list.

Although these things can get HILARIOUS, they will quickly show you (and potential clients) why you are the perfect match for who they are as people...or why they would be a total waste of your time.

Here are my "Top 10 Reasons You Should Never Work With Me" as inspiration for you.

1. You're scared of bold action.
2. You want to keep playing small.
3. You like to take it slow.
4. You're not confident in your skills.
5. You don't like loving kicks in the butt.
6. Unwavering support and guidance don't float your boat.
7. You desire hand holding or someone to do it for you.
8. You have all the time in the world.
9. I'm too straightforward.
10. You're comfortable with ground level and aren't looking for the next step.

The fact is, if you work with me, I'm going to push you to reach your full potential. God didn't put me in anyone's life to just stand by and watch them drown in mediocrity. If someone prefers that mediocrity, they should never work with me.

Like I said at the beginning of this chapter, selling without sleaze is ALL about knowing the value of what you provide, then standing by that value before, during and after every launch.

Whether you are aiming for 1,000 new customers for your next product launch or you'll be happy with 10 new 1:1 services clients, make it your mission to do one thing exceedingly well:

Transfer YOUR enthusiasm for your offering from your world, to your prospect's.

THAT is the mark of good salesmanship—and the mark of a profitable business.

You'll never spot a successful entrepreneur without it.

CHAPTER 8

Raves, Repeats and Referrals

Shameless self-promotion is the crux of growing your online personal brand. But when other people talk and rave about you, you can literally take that to the bank.

When I say, "Organic Growth" what comes to mind?

Anything from eating literal organic fruits and veggies, to growing your business without spending money on ads, I bet.

For the sake of this book, I will stick with the second of the two. (Although I do love my organic green smoothies!)

Before we step through the eighth and final doorway to freedom, it makes sense to define my terms first.

From *The Jenn Scalia Dictionary Of Business*:

Organic Growth (ȯr-ˈga-nik grōTH): *To increase your customer base and profit margins by creating an army of raving fans, turning one-time customers into repeat buyers and earning referrals from everyone you know*

RAVES, REPEATS AND REFERRALS

If you can spend $10 to make $100, do it.

But if you can spend $0 to make $100, DEFI-NITELY do it.

In this last chapter, I am going to show you how—by implementing Organic Growth in YOUR business, AKA Raves, Repeats and Referrals.

Creating an army of raving fans, turning one-time customers into repeat buyers and earning referrals from everyone you know requires integrity.

It's been said that integrity is the foremost of all the virtues, because upon it, all others stand.

The same goes for Organic Growth. Yes, you want to be known as an influencer in your niche, but without ethics and conscious choices to abide by them even when it's difficult, you can kiss the 3 R's goodbye.

That doesn't mean you need to be as "nice" as possible to anyone and everyone who flirts with the outer edges of your Tribe. I want you to be SO authentic and real that you weed out people who aren't for you so you can attract more of those who will really connect with you.

You CAN come from a place of service without sacrificing who you truly are.

And when you do, customers become raving fans. First-time buyers buy again and again and again. And your network cannot seem to STOP sending new business your way.

Organic Growth, Check!

YOUR FIRST SIX FIGURES

The simplest aspect of Organic Growth—think of it as the tiny seed of a flowering plant—is the customer experience you offer.

Want people to rave about you? Give them something rave-worthy!

Authentic leaders treat everyone who enters their Tribe with the same level of appreciation, whether it's Client #1 whose transaction is worth $5,000 or Customer #3,087 whose transaction is worth $47.

So, how DO you show your customers that you appreciate them?

Frankly, it has very little to do with your product or service itself. Instead, it's about HOW you deliver that product or service.

What do your onboarding and off-boarding procedures look like?

Do your clients know exactly what to expect every step of the way? Are you regularly reminding them why they joined your program or decided to work with you? Do they feel like you want their feedback at every stage?

As humans, we want to feel like the people we trust are looking out for us. That's why in addition to onboarding and off-boarding procedures, you want to introduce both systems and accountability into the customer experience.

For systems, I'm talking about using the latest software and processes to make it EASY to work with you.

RAVES, REPEATS AND REFERRALS

Don't make clients fill out paper forms, fax them over to you, print off documents or track their progress manually.

Tools like Basecamp, Slack, Moovia or Asana are excellent collaborative project management software systems to create an unforgettably smooth customer experience for service-based clients.

And don't make members of your programs guess where to go next and what to do when they get there either.

If you have to, hire a Virtual Assistant who touches base with your members every couple of days. Use plugins or extensions on your website to let customers mark their progress and receive reminders as they work their way through each learning module.

As you can see, the best systems for managing clients and customers has accountability built in—from checklists to to-do's to automated reminders.

But the most important aspect of accountability isn't written in code—it's written on the hearts of your customers.

When you show your Tribe that you care SO much about their success that you're willing to call them out on procrastination or half-assery, they cannot HELP but respect—and yes, *love*—you for it.

Following these tips, you will find your customer base transforming into an army of raving fans who are THRILLED to buy from you again.

That just makes sense, doesn't it?

Jo buys X Product. She loves it. AND she loves the experience.

So, Jo buys Y Product from the same company. Again, she LOVES it.

Turning one-off transactions into multiple ones is as easy as providing an experience the very first time around that makes buyers go, "DAMN! This woman is going all-out for me!"

Even if you have a single signature program or only one primary service, you can enjoy the perks of new business from your client base.

I don't mean just repeat business—I'm talking referrals!

For example, my 1:1 Coaching spots are ALWAYS filled despite the fact I do ZERO marketing or paid advertising for that service.

Why?

Because 1 month in, 2 months in, 6 months in...

The results speak for themselves.

I leverage the most advanced systems, have foolproof procedures and keep my clients in check with (at times) ruthless accountability.

Therefore, it's only NATURAL that my clients experience the results I promise—so OF COURSE they tell everyone in their circles to get on the waiting list!

I've even had a client who had a client who had a client who had a client...and ALL of them joined my 1:1 Coaching program!

RAVES, REPEATS AND REFERRALS

Organic Growth for the win!

I also like to supplement these spontaneous referrals with gentle reminders of my own.

It's NEVER a bad idea to ask your customers and clients for referrals—unless you suck at what you do. (Since you're reading this book, I know that's not the case.)

Ask yourself, "Why do I deserve to receive referrals?"

Brainstorm a few answers, then wordsmith those ideas into your authentic requests to your customer base.

Something like, "Because you've gotten results XYZ, who else do you know who wants those results, too?" is an excellent start!

You can even sweeten the pot and offer a 10-20% finder's fee for any referral you receive that turns into a client.

Yet another way to show your peeps how much you appreciate them.

As with referrals, it's a smart move to get into the habit of providing your customers with SUCH an amazing experience that they feel like they OWE you testimonials.

I am NOT referring to those total bullshit "This person is great! I highly recommend her. 5/5 stars!" reviews though.

You want testimonials that tell the story of WHY your clients chose you, WHY they enjoyed your product or service and WHY they continue to believe it was worth paying for.

You can request testimonials through a feedback survey or directly in an email to your customer or client base.

Include something like this in your testimonial request emails:

I would love if you could send me a few lines telling me how much you enjoyed working with me and how it has transformed your business. To make it easier, you can answer these questions specifically:

- *How were you feeling before we started our work together?*
- *What made you sign up for the program?*
- *Were you happy with your decision?*
- *How did this program transform your business and/or your knowledge & skill level? Please give specific results (like # of clients, # of consults, business or visibility growth, places you were published in, etc.)*
- *How do you feel now about your business?*
- *What's been the best part of working with me?*
- *If a friend were thinking of working with me, what would you tell them?*

Referrals and testimonials are a double-edged sword that allows your brand to cut through the noise so people know, like and trust you LONG before they consider buying your first product. Always choose impact over noise.

In a world where 500,000+ new businesses are started every. single. month. you cannot afford to pass up on the Organic Growth that referrals and testimonials offer.

But like I said at the beginning of this chapter, you only want people who are RIGHT for you entertaining the idea of joining your Tribe.

You're not for everyone. And that means you have to decide who your products and services are DEFINITELY not for.

We dug into this a little bit in Chapter 7 with the "Reasons Not To Work With Me" list.

Now, I want you to think more strategically about HOW you will stand out and magnetize your true Tribe—the people destined to become raving fans—while REPELLING everyone else.

Reflect a bit on how you want your brand to polarize. Ask yourself:

- What can I do to stand out and attract my "soulmate" clients?
- Who do I exclusively serve?
- What accomplishments do I have in life and/or business that make me uniquely suited to serve these people?
- Is there anything out of alignment? Is there anything I am asking my clients to do that I have not yet done myself?

These questions drive the strategy of exclusivity marketing, where the general public cannot misconstrue who you will and will not work with.

For example, Ramit Sethi of *I Will Teach You To Be Rich* and GrowthLab.com prohibits anyone with credit card debt from entering any of his flagship programs.

Instead, Ramit makes it VERY clear that aspiring customers of his should implement his free material FIRST to pay off their debts, then join when they're ready and meet his requirement.

That is influence with integrity. My standards are more on the qualitative side of things, as I prohibit excuse-makers who expect codependency from their coach from joining any of my programs.

I have even had to tell people face-to-face during a discovery call, "Sorry, I will not work with someone like you. Have a great day. *<End Call>*"

Were they pissed? You bet!

But I believe in taking a stand. I believe in adhering to a strict code of ethics.

And I believe in influencing with integrity. THAT creates respect for you in the marketplace.

Now, I am not implying that your homework in this chapter is to copy Ramit's and my approach to exclusivity marketing.

The standards you live your daily life with— what you expect from *yourself*—those are the fuel that powers your own exclusivity marketing.

For me, it wasn't until I got in total alignment with who I could help and who I couldn't that things actually started falling into place.

Once I decided what my standards would be, I had a new joy and excitement when I talked to others about my business. I wanted people to know what I did, I wanted to shout it from the rooftops, I knew that I could help people get results.

RAVES, REPEATS AND REFERRALS

THAT is when my Tribe of 1,000 True Fans manifested itself.

By taking a stand, I've gotten noticed by influencers who, years earlier, I could NEVER have imagined looking up to me—much less even looking AT me!

Now, my Tribe includes many of the influencers I once wanted to mentor ME.

My business has skyrocketed as a result. One influencer asked me to be her right-hand coach and co-manage her group of over 10,000 female entrepreneurs. We are now in cahoots to host multiple courses and podcasts together.

Another influencer invited me to speak at her event in New York City, where 200 passionate entrepreneurs gather every year to learn from the best and brightest in the business.

And a third influencer invited me to mastermind with her in Bali and become part of her inner circle of client advisors. How cool is that?

Now, these aren't small time players, they are the REAL DEAL. They saw me playing BIG, and they noticed.

The same goes with my Tribe of clients and customers, which now numbers in the TENS of thousands.

Since launching *Captivate*, I've had the honor of giving my star students a platform to show off their success to THOUSANDS of people.

Side note there—one of the fastest ways to become an influencer is to *get noticed* by one. Apply yourself to the programs and courses you've already bought from them, and you can see your face next to theirs all over the internet.

The fact is, real recognizes real.

Passion magnetizes the passionate.

My personal drive to always be the best made all of this possible.

And it can for you, too.

So go out there and be the best.

You will stand out and you will get noticed.

And you will be on the receiving end of more raves, repeats and referrals than you know what to do with.

Why waste your time doing anything less?

CONCLUSION

Are You Coming With Me?

The doors are open...

The way is clear...

Freedom is at hand!

Are you coming with me?

You would be surprised how many people receive an invitation like this—yet say, "No."

The fact is, freedom can be scary.

...to someone who's never experienced it before.

Freedom is hard.

...to someone who's never felt the 4 walls of a cubicle close in on them.

Freedom brings insecurity.

...to someone who's never been laid off, broke and single.

For seeking freedom without shame or worry, some have called me crazy.

YOUR FIRST SIX FIGURES

What can I say?

I just like the Light.

The Darkness of other people's expectations, other people's ideas and other people's advice clouded my view of myself and my view of my potential for FAR too long.

Now that you have received the 8 keys of freedom—and have before you 8 doorways to it—I want one sentence to be on your lips, directed at the naysayers who come (they always do).

"F you!"

This is YOUR life we're talking about here!

Have you ever seen a wild animal set free from a cage, then forced back inside it for whatever reason?

The animal's hatred for that prison is FAR worse the second time—because it's seen freedom. It's felt it.

Now the creature knows what it's missing out on.

Sister, I REFUSE to let that be you.

Hell, that's why I wrote this book in the first place!

And that's why this Conclusion is more so a Call-To-Action.

Maybe you see someone as loud and proud as I am in my business and wonder, "Can I ever be like her someday?"

Look, I'm an INTJ according to the Myers-Briggs

ARE YOU COMING WITH ME?

Type Indicator®—the rarest of all personality types, making up fewer than 1% of women on the planet.

In other words, I'm a master builder. Intuitive. Methodical. A strategist. An objective thinker. A succinct writer.

And most importantly, **defiant of authority**.

If there's anyone you want in your corner, it's someone who can turn up their nose at the powers-that-be, the experts who get it wrong, the naysayers who give you every reason you can't (when we both know you CAN).

But it's YOUR drive to succeed that is your vehicle to follow every lesson, every tip and every strategy I've laid out for you.

I'll ride shotgun and give directions, but it's your job to drive.

To do your due diligence.

To do the work.

One of the BIGGEST mistakes I see new entrepreneurs (and even seasoned ones) make, is get excited about their potential to build multiple streams of revenue and leave a lasting legacy for their family...

Then skip the essentials.

Don't be that girl.

Don't skip the market research. Don't skip the content creation. Don't skip the long-term list-building techniques. Don't skip the new product surveys.

YOUR FIRST SIX FIGURES

The last thing I want for you is to miscarry your dreams.

So keep the non-negotiables, *non-negotiable*.

Otherwise, you'll feel yourself sucked into the world of the wantrepreneur, where "Now" becomes "Someday", "I did" becomes "When I", "I choose to invest" becomes "I can't afford it" and "I am committed" becomes "I don't have the time".

Remember, hoping is not acting.

Praying is not doing.

Learning is not implementing.

It boggles my mind how many would-be success stories are trying to launch businesses without the clarity they need, the single-mindedness of "whatever it takes".

Like Marie Forleo says, "Clarity comes from engagement, not thought." You've got to put ACTION behind your ideas.

I'm NOT talking about action that gets you nowhere, like diddling around on Facebook, printing new business cards or redesigning your entry-level product's color scheme for the seventeenth time.

You have to KNOW what you're working towards and why, or else you'll always be on a perpetual search for something more.

"I want to be a millionaire" doesn't cut it. Focus not on the results, but the *process*.

ARE YOU COMING WITH ME?

Be the type of person who *automatically* gets the results you want—whether it's a million bucks in the bank, a comfortable living for your family or an income to replace the 9-to-5.

When it comes to talk of money and profit, I need to reiterate something one final time:

There's no one-size-fits-all for success.

If your goal is to simply earn an extra $2,000-$3,000 per month on the side to pay off student loans, OWN it!

Don't compare yourself to role models or to peers.

No one is like you. No one.

There is no comparison, and there is no competition. We are all unique in our own right, and we all have something different to bring to the table.

I'm not bullshitting you, this is really true.

When I first started business coaching, I had another coach approach me for a Joint Venture. I didn't want to follow through at first because I thought we were too similar in our message.

Against my better judgment, I decided to work with her, and by doing so, I realized how different we really were. Her potential clients definitely weren't mine.

That's why I now truly believe that the people you are meant to help will find you, and it will happen the way it's supposed to.

But you've got to SHOW UP.

YOUR FIRST SIX FIGURES

Put in the work.

And give, give, give, give, give.

This book is meant to be the fuel that launches you into orbit—but it's your own drive that will take you the rest of the way to your destination.

So don't expect the Universe to come to you if you're not willing to meet it halfway.

And don't expect to achieve the results of a master when you're an apprentice.

In college, you don't graduate after taking one class. An A+ grade on your first exam does not earn you a degree straightaway.

You take multiple classes, including prerequisites, before you are even allowed to take classes relevant to your field of study. You go for years and years—sometimes 2, sometimes 4, sometimes 8.

You have multiple teachers in multiple areas of studies. And often you even attend more than one school. Then after all the study and all that hard work, you are FINALLY eligible to receive your diploma or degree.

The same is true for business. You don't take one program. Or work with one coach and expect 6 or 7 figures. You work through multiple areas of study and take lots of different programs or courses on different things. (In the Bonus Chapter, I'll provide several resources for you to accelerate your education—and the results that come with it.)

There is no magic pill or one-size-fits-all remedy for success.

ARE YOU COMING WITH ME?

True success comes from mastery in all areas—business, finances, life, relationships and mindset.

Think about that before you claim that a certain strategy or book didn't work. I have yet to take a course (and I've taken *dozens*) or work with a coach (at least 10) where I walked away having learned absolutely NOTHING or grown even a little bit.

Why?

Because I realized something.

Trying to block out the voices of the naysayers while stumbling about in the Darkness, I discovered a truth that freed me from the scourge of their lies:

"I am in control of my destiny—I am the ONLY one in control of my destiny."

And so are you.

You are in control of what you choose to implement—and the results you enjoy because of it.

You are in control of which doorways to freedom you walk through—all of them or none of them.

And **you are in control** of the way you view the world—is it your oyster, or the big bad wolf?

(Here we are getting into mindset again, finishing where we started.)

With your new Operating System, the world already looks different to you.

From this day forward, shift the way you see the work you're going to be doing to implement what I've taught you.

Don't think of it as "work"—start calling it "love".

Think of what you do, as things that you LOVE doing.

For example, I call my own work "love" because:

- I **love** connecting with new people.
- I **love** creating content.
- I **love** changing people's lives.
- I **love** helping people make money.
- I **love** creating images and quotes.
- I **love** figuring things out.
- I **love** being a leader.
- I **love** making my own schedule.
- I **love** sleeping in.
- I **love** being able to spend a lot of time with my son.
- I **love** being debt free.
- I **love** dreaming bigger.
- I **love** intellectual conversations.
- I **love** being around like-minded women.
- I **love** thinking outside of the box.
- I **love** giving others inspiration.
- I **love** turning dreams into reality.
- I **love** sharing my story.

When you commit to finding what you love in the midst of the work you're already doing—or about to do—you completely change your entrepreneurial trajectory.

From railroad tie to hockey stick—THAT much of a change.

ARE YOU COMING WITH ME?

Are you okay with revenue growth that, on a chart, is as flat as a railroad tie?

I'm not.

Are you okay with just getting by, snagging a new sale here and a new sale there?

I'm not.

Are you okay with living an ordinary life and owning an ordinary business?

I'm not.

Even if you're feeling overwhelmed about the journey ahead, keep taking action.

Because confidence comes from action.

More action, in turn, builds more confidence.

And so, this beautiful, mystical, actual cycle of success continues.

It's a cycle that I've been enjoying for YEARS now.

4 figures of income became 5.

...became 6.

...became 7.

It is with this reality in one hand that I extend to you the other:

Are you coming with me?

BONUS CHAPTER

Expand Your Mind

(And Bank Account)

Women who invest in themselves go further.

Ready for the world to know your name?

I've got you covered, sister.

You've learned SO much from this book so far, and you're ready to start implementing—and getting results.

As your journey continues, you will be ready for new classes, new lessons.

...and the results that come with them.

You're going to be hustling hard to build the life and business of your dreams.

You'll try your hardest to avoid shiny objects and stick with that ONE thing that finally works for you.

With my 8 keys in hand, you're dreaming about unlimited earning potential, financial freedom and time to do the things you actually LOVE. . .with the people you love.

I know you want to change people's lives, get your message out there and do the work that lights you up.

The only thing is, there's a tiny little (read: giant) problem we're all facing. Maybe you've already spotted it:

Saturation.

While I love the fact that this book is being read by thousands of people, it's possible that at least a handful of them are in your industry and work with your ideal clients.

What does this often lead to?

Self-doubt. Confusion. Overwhelm.

Yes, your new Operating System can help with that.

But if you want to generate sustainable income in a saturated industry, you CANNOT do it without a PROVEN strategy.

If you want to get out of the feast or famine cycle and stop feeling like "just another" coach, mentor or service provider, you CANNOT do it without changing your BUSINESS MODEL to one that aligns with you.

You have what it takes to make it, because you've come this far, and there's no way in hell you are giving up now -- especially not since you have my 8 keys in your pocket!

YOUR FIRST SIX FIGURES

So if you're ready to take what you've learned here to the next level and stand out in a notoriously crowded industry and become a POWERHOUSE leader. . .

And if you're ready to go from overlooked to fully booked by creating an audience of people who want to buy from you over and over again...

Send an email to **yourfirstsixfigures@gmail. com** OR visit **yourfirstsixfigures.com** to receive a FREE gift to help you:

- Create a movement
- Discover how to stand out in your industry
- Undergo an unstoppable transformation that cannot be ignored by clients, competitors or fans

Get ready to take MASSIVE action and become the BEST you can be.

Because if you're not trying to be the best, what are you even doing?

About the Author

Jenn Scalia is a visibility strategist for entrepreneurs who want the world to know their name. A self-professed introvert and single mom, Jenn went from rock bottom to building a 7-figure business in less than 3 years.

Today, Jenn teaches women entrepreneurs how to captivate their audiences, create raving fans, maximize their impact and make more sales through her popular programs and trainings, including *The Little Black Business Book*, *Captivate*, *Continuity Rocks*, *Five Figure Funnels*, and *Wealth From Within*.

Jenn's tough love, no-B.S. business wisdom has appeared in *Fast Company, Forbes, Entrepreneur, INC, Success, Business Insider, YFS Magazine, Entrepreneur on Fire, Inspired Coach, FarnooshTV, Social Media Marketing World, MindBodyGreen* and numerous other outlets.

After co-authoring the bestselling book *Against the Grain* with Brian Tracy in 2013, Jenn traced back her journey from unemployed professional to struggling solopreneur to multiple six-figure online business owner so she could share everything she learned along the way. The result of five years of self-reflection is her second book, *Your First Six Figures: Eight Keys to Unlock Freedom, Flow and Financial Success with Your Online Business*, published in February 2018.

Learn more Jenn, her books and her programs at www.JennScalia.com.